W9-BDD-600

Endorsements

"This is a refreshing, challenging, highly practical book that will be very helpful in showing people how to live in the presence of Jesus each day."

Wayne Grudem, Ph.D.,
Research Professor of Theology and Biblical Studies
Phoenix Seminary, Phoenix, Arizona

"The only imperative in Jesus' Great Commission is to make disciples. This book goes a long way in enabling us to understand the meaning of discipleship as a way of life. With richness of Scripture, suggestions for reflection and daily practices, this is an exceptional tool for personal, small group and church use. I highly recommend it."

Dennis P. Hollinger, Ph.D.,
President and
Colman M. Mockler Distinguished Professor of Christian Ethics,
Gordon-Conwell Theological Seminary

"The Five Stones will encourage transformative and Christ-centered discipleship, as well as the strengthening of churches, small groups, individuals and families. I am pleased to recommend this fine book."

David S. Dockery, Ph.D.,
President Trinity International University

"The Five Stones presents a challenge to move beyond knowledge and into practice. The authors desire implementation and not just information. I commend them and share the desire to see a generation live out their faith for

God and our nation revived. I encourage you not only to read this book, but to live a life sold out to Jesus."

Thomas White,
President, Cedarville University

"People who are serious about doing real discipleship with real people in the real world need to read "The Five Stones Primer". Foye and Sam have done an excellent job outlining an approach to discipleship that is both biblical and practical. Their work is clear and insightful, as well as passionate and full of conviction. The Christian life is much more than a set of doctrinal beliefs or an assertion of faith. The Christian life is to be lived. This book inspires and instructs Christians to live that life as Jesus intended."

Todd J. Williams, Ph.D.,
President, Cairn University

"Huggard and Belyea have written a much needed Biblical and practical guide for Christ followers who desire to live out the life of being centered in Christ and sent by Christ. I enjoyed and was challenged by the clear Scriptural teaching on what it means to be a disciple. Healthy transformational churches are built on disciples and disciplemakers but the evidence is clear that most churches are not seeing an increased number of disciples. I believe we need to get back to the "Five Stones" so clearly described in this book."

William Hamel,
President of EFCA

"The simple call of discipleship is to live in obedience to Jesus. Foye Belyea and Sam Huggard provide practical insight into this way of life by providing guide stones as markers to an effective Christian life. These guide stones help the reader prioritize kingdom values and live in the presence and power of Jesus."

Dr. Ron Hamilton, D. Min.,
Conference Minister,
Conservative Congregational Christian Conference

"So many in the church today make following Christ so mysterious and complicated that it's easy to lose heart and feel like you're not a very good follower of Jesus. The truth is, the Bible shows us how to become passionate followers of Christ. The Bible reveals our new identity and freedom in Christ. The Five Stones is all about discovering simple Biblical truths that make following Jesus easily understandable. Enjoy this great little book and don't leave any stone unturned."

Dave Park,
President Infusion Ministries, co-Author of *Stomping out The Darkness and the Bondage Breaker Youth Edition*

"The world today as well as the church are demanding that the way of Jesus be lived out in and through our lives and not just something we talk about. *The Five Stones* powerfully and practically addresses what it means to live out the way of Jesus beginning in our own lives, our families and in our churches. Beginning with the scriptures, the authors provide everyday practices that are especially effective for marriages and families, which people in the church today desperately need. I believe this book will

help raise up a new generation of Christ-followers and disciplemakers who will transform families, church, communities and the world."

Fritz Dale,
Executive Director, Reach National, EFCA

"In Acts, Luke reported that those on the path of following
Jesus were on "the Way." Much later J.R.R. Tolkien added that not all who wander are lost. Today many on "the
Way" say they wander because they feel lost. Read this
book and two things happen: you actually find yourself in
the geography of the Kingdom, and you experience the
companionship of fellow Christ-followers, Sam and Foye,
who teach you how to journey with Jesus in community."

Gary G. Hoag, Ph.D.,
NT scholar, author, and professor

"There is a lot of discussion today among church leaders
about the importance of making disciples. What's missing
are actual practitioners—people who are living a lifestyle
of disciple making. What I love about this book is that it is
not offering theory but rather practices that actually work.
Implement the insights from this book and watch the impact of your life significantly increase."

Alan Kraft,
Author of *More: When a Little Bit of the Spirit is Not Enough*,
and Pastor of Christ Community Church

"*The Five Stones* is a homerun for discipleship in the family context and in the context of the church, specifically
small group. The result of this discipleship will be missional
communities. In the New Testament the Way is a person,

the Truth is a person, and the Life is the person of Jesus. Thus, in a life on life context of family and small groups the five stones create an environment centered in Jesus of study and applying the Word, learning to follow the Holy Spirit, engaging in family worship, developing disciplines of devotion and rest, as well as intentionally advancing the Kingdom together. Powerful and transformative. A game winning homer, I would say."

Ves Sheely,
NEDA, Superintendent, New England District Association, EFCA

"In the Great Commission of Matthew 28, Jesus commands His followers to make more disciples who can do all that He has commanded. This is the heart of our mission — to pass on the way of Jesus to others. This is both a lost emphasis and forgotten art in the Church in the West. *The Five Stones* provides disciple-makers a practical, biblically-based process for fulfilling the commission of Jesus. This is a tool you need if you are serious about fulfilling Jesus' mandate for you to engage and make more disciples for Him."

Tom Johnston,
pastor, author, educator and Executive Director of
The Praxis Center for Church Development

"Jesus has continued to fascinate people and his way of life has been compelling in every generation. The challenge to effective ministry often comes down to the fact that we substitute institutions and methods for an authentic incarnation of Jesus. *The Five Stones* is a much needed call (to me and every other Christ follower) to remember a practical way of life that leads us toward Jesus. The five stones point to a way of life that can restore our churches of every size and kind into transforming families of faith."

Jeff Sorvik,
Church Multiplication Catalyst, EFCA

"Every once in a while you hold something in your hands and you know deep down it is a good gift from a very Good God. That's how I feel about The Five Stones. Through process, experience and practice a group of families set out on an life-long adventure and mined for us five stones that you'll soon find out are absolute gems. I know these guys, I've seen their lives, I've met their families and I can attest to the fruit that has emerged from a very simple yet intentional way of life. My family has been personally impacted by their lives and their work. My highest recommendations to dig into this book."

Kevin Colón,
Neighboring Life, LifeBridge Christian Church

"The Five Stones is a dangerous read. It is great in the busy world that we live in to find a gem that is not only worth the time but also very encouraging. This book made me laugh, cry and contemplate my walk with Christ. I encourage readers to 'proceed with caution.' The Five Stones will be a great resource for the body of Christ in the days to come!"

Rev. Gregory Dyson,
Director of Intercultural Leadership, Cedarville University

"Whether developing a new church plant or revitalizing an existing congregation, the non-negotiable key is always making disciples. Discipleship is a buzzword today in many Christian circles, but too often it is equated more with providing information than fostering transformation. Five Stones is an incredible tool to both explain and lead people through truly transformative discipleship. I cannot recommend it more highly."

Dr. John Kimball,
Director of Church Development for the
Conservative Congregational Christian Conference

"*The Five Stones* is not about how to change your church through refreshed or innovative programming. Rather than focusing on the structures of the church, the authors instead set their aim on helping everyday people embrace a way of life in Christ resulting in greater intimacy with Jesus and imitation of Jesus. *The Five Stones* provides simple and accessible practices in how to follow Jesus together in everyday life."

Shane Stacey,
Director of ReachStudents, EFCA

"I thank God for Evangelical Free Church pastors! They are faithful to the gospel and students of the culture. Most importantly, they have a passion to make disciples. Not content to debate theology in the seminaries, Free Church leaders write great books for people in the pew and pastors in the trenches. *The Five Stones* is one of them. Bill Hull's disciple-making books impacted thousands of us a generation ago. *The Five Stones* may have a similar impact today. I especially appreciate the emphasis on listening to the Spirit and Sabbath keeping, themes which are often overlooked in discipleship materials. Well done!"

Doug Banister,
Pastor, All Souls Church, Knoxville, TN

"Anytime some guys get together to intentionally spur one another in following Jesus it's a good thing! It is an even a better thing when they share the lessons they have been learning while in that community of fellow Christ-followers. Read this book for practical 'how to' insights on ways to strengthen your community as a follower of Jesus."

Brad Brinson,
Senior Pastor, Two Rivers Church, Knoxville, TN

"This book is a TREASURE! There are a lot of books about disciple making. This one is unpretentiously different. It is like a personal journal and practical like a getting started manual. This book also weaves three strings of thought about life that should mingle organically but are rarely united: the disciple making way of Jesus for today, the partnership of the Holy Spirit in this endeavor, and finally living it all out in the intentional rhythms of life in this day that shuns fakes. I am Hispanic and know that I don't have to contextualize this for my community because these hermanos are already speaking our relational language. As a pastor this is the second book I will introduce the people of my church to after the Bible. I know that *The Five Stones* will help me guide them to and in the WAY! - Yo también soy un arquitecto."

Alejandro (Alex) Mandes, D.Min.,
Director of Immigrant Mission EFCA
Executive Director of Immigrant Hope

"Thankfully, the Five Stones is not a program. It is a very readable and understandable guide for living life as a disciple of Christ and encouraging others to do the same. Discipleship needs to be lived out ever day, not trotted out as a means to grow your church. This is the most practical book I have read on the subject. It helps put into practice what we have known in theory."

Rev. Terry H Shanahan,
Northeast Regional Minister
Conservative Congregational Christian Conference

"*The Five Stones* easily finds its way into my backpack as a practical, adaptable disciplemaking implement. Sam and Foye's useful metaphor connects biblical principles to their real life values. It's helping me to communicate those principles in more captivating ways. In *The Five Stones* my disciplemaking journey has found a new and effective traveling companion."

Glen Schrieber,
Superintendent, EFCA Southeast

"Foye and Sam are both passionate men of God with a deep longing to see the Church live out its faith in the day to day reality of life. This passion has given rise to this delightful work that seeks to develop saints that love God with all that they are, love others as they love themselves and as they live life, make disciples. The beauty and simplicity of their thoughts will invite the reader to not settle for a life of mundane religious behaviors, but follow the path of the five stones that will lead to a life of fullness where love is a lived reality and joy and peace are present companions."

Mike Chong Perkinson,
Lead Pastor of New Heights Boise, ID, Senior Developer of
The Praxis Center for Church Development

"Foye Belyea and Sam Huggard have made it simple. Starting with the call to live—really live—in God's kingdom and working through the Great Commandment and the Great Commission, all the way to how to spend a day in God's presence and to understanding the "sent-ness" we all have because of our relationship with Jesus, Foye & Sam lay out a simple roadmap to making lots and lots of disciples of the King. It's amazing how far you can go with five simple stones! Let Foye Belyea and Sam Huggard show you how."

Jonathan Reitz,
Director of Training/CEO, CoachNet

"The contemporary church craves simplicity but is reluctant to trust it. It longs to transform the world but struggles in the essential work of making disciples. These men offer a simple path for disciple making that is adorned with wisdom and a richness forged from their own obedience. Take the path! Walk in its counsel! Let it help you discover your own path. Then repeat!"

Larry Austin,
Director of Church Health, EFCA Central

The Five Stones
An Everyday Guide To Following Jesus

The Five Stones

An Everyday Guide to Following Jesus

by

Foye Belyea & Samuel Huggard

Foreword by Bill Hull

NEXTSTEP RESOURCES

The Five Stones
An Everyday Guide To Following Jesus
Copyright © Foye Belyea & Samuel Huggard
All rights reserved.

No part of this book may be used or reproduced stored in a retrieval system, or transmitted in any form or by any means—electronic, mechanical, photocopy, recording, or any other manner—without the prior written permission from the author, except in case of brief quotations embodied in critical articles and reviews.

While all stories in this book are true, some names and identifying information in this book have been changed to protect the privacy of the individuals involved.

Unless otherwise indicated, all Scripture quotations are from The Holy Bible, English Standard Version® (ESV®), copyright © 2001 by Crossway, a publishing ministry of Good News Publishers.
Used by permission. All rights reserved.

(NLT) Scripture quotations are taken from the Holy Bible, New Living Translation, copyright ©1996, 2004, 2007, 2013 by Tyndale House Foundation. Used by permission of Tyndale House Publishers, Inc., Carol Stream, Illinois 60188.
All rights reserved

ISBN: 978-0-911802-81-8

Published in the United States of America
by
NextStep Resources
7890 12th Ave South Minneapolis, MN 55425
(800) 444-2665

Design, Layout and Format: Kim Gardell, Graphic Design

Table of Contents

Foreword

In 1976 I became the pastor at an Evangelical Free church in Laguna Hills, California. I had been schooled to believe that the heart of church work was to make disciples, but there were very few examples as to how to go about it. I started simply by calling my Christian parishioners disciples. It made more sense to me to do so because "disciple" was used 269 times in the New Testament and "Christian" a paltry three times. The name change got their attention, but it took me years to figure out how to go about making disciples.

The greatest challenge was to convince the ordinary disciple that they could actually do something special with God. It took me seven years to learn how to talk about it, learn how to live it myself, and learn how to teach it. I then felt the strongest compulsion to write a book. It was obvious where I was to begin: with the simple claim that Jesus made disciples, and we should pay attention to how he did it.

Countless reader responses and challenges to the book, *Jesus Christ, Disciplemaker,* eventually led to a second book, *The Disciple-Making Pastor,* which grabbed the attention of the academic and pastoral worlds, as it asserts that disciple-making should be first priority for the pastor. Critics followed with the claim that Jesus' disciples didn't do discipleship, which—you guessed it—led to a third book, *The Disciple-Making Church,* which contends that discipleship must be the focus of every disciple.

After three books in six years, I found myself traveling the world as a discipleship evangelist, calling the church to choose the life of following Jesus. Now, after 38 years as a discipleship evangelist, God has seen fit to place discipleship front and center in the mind of his church. The long struggle for the church's attentiveness to discipleship has been like a long train ride. When I got on, Robert Coleman, author of The Master Plan of Evangelism, was already aboard, as were leaders such as Carl Wilson, Howard Ball, Leroy Eims, and Elton Trueblood. I have seen much from the windows and learned a great deal from many stops along the way, and now I am glad that Foye Belyea and Sam Huggard are joining us with The Five Stones. Every author who hops on board brings a new perspective, fresh words, and unique life experience for their time and Foye and Sam are certainly no exception. I wholeheartedly commend their important work to you.

I like this book. *The Five Stones* has a good vibe, it feels right to me, and I like its heart. Belyea and Huggard cover the crucial issues of what it means to be a follower of Jesus in a holistic and relationally satisfying way. Clearly, they have walked the path they lay out in the following pages, so rest assured that you are being led along by experienced guides. As you travel with them from stone to stone, be sure to pay special attention to the vertical and horizontal practices they outline, which are crucial insights for the discipleship journey. From "SASHET" to Sabbath, and from family worship to missional living—all of which you will learn about in the coming pages—you simply cannot go wrong with *The Five Stones'* scripture-saturated, everyday approach to following Jesus.

While all of the insights found herein are profound, perhaps what is most important in their book is not plainly stated, albeit crucial: They have a healthy gospel. I can tell without them saying it. What I mean is it covers all of life, not just getting your sins forgiven and getting into heaven. A healthy gospel—the only true gospel, really—is upheld here, as Foye and Sam guide disciples in ". . . walk[ing] in a manner worthy of the calling to which [they] have been called" (Eph. 4:1).

In my opinion, the most crucial issue facing the contemporary church is the nature of our gospel. What does the gospel we preach naturally lead to? If our gospel is forgiveness only, then discipleship is only an option, not an expectation. The whole point of being a disciple is to become like Jesus. If our gospel caters to our needs only, if it is focused on consumerism, making sure we get all our perceived needs met through the church, then there is no way we can become Christlike. If we try to make Christlike disciples based on a contemporary consumeristic gospel, we will fail! The reason is simple: The contemporary consumeristic gospel is about us, and Jesus is about others.

To be Christlike is to live for others and to allow that process to meet your needs as a by-product.

It is abundantly clear throughout *The Five Stones* that the authors have not fallen prey to a contemporary gospel lacking in substance; rather, they present a guide to following Jesus which is grounded in historic, orthodox faith, while remaining organic in its approach. If you're looking for something fluffy that's going to keep you comfortable in the complacency of an anemic gospel, then look elsewhere. However, if you are looking to be challenged in your faith and to dig down deep in fertile soil, then look no further. Evidently, Foye and Sam believe that Jesus is aboard the discipleship train, and I pray that God would use *The Five Stones*, with its roots in a healthy gospel, to motivate many more to travel with us along the way and encounter the full life found only in following Jesus.

Bill Hull,
Founder, The Bonhoeffer Project,
Author of: *Conversion and Discipleship,*
You Can't Have One Without the Other,
December 2014

Introduction

If a friend or co-worker asked you today what it looks like to follow Jesus, how would you answer? Would you define the facts and doctrines you *KNOW*? Would you describe the religious services you *ATTEND*? Would you list the ministry activities you *PERFORM*?

While gaining Bible knowledge, attending worship gatherings, and performing ministry activities are good, even necessary aspects of the Christian life, they are incomplete by themselves to define what it means to follow Jesus. We can know and agree with all the right facts about Jesus, regularly attend a church service, and even participate in ministry, yet still not follow Jesus in our everyday lives.

If we are to live the Christian life that God intends, we must recapture what Jesus' first followers understood: following Jesus is about a way of life that is lived in the everyday. Jesus called His first followers to a way of life with Him, like Him, for Him, and by Him. These first followers were not initially known as "Christians" but "followers of the Way" or "those who belonged to the Way" (Acts 9:2,

22:4-5, 24:14). This "Way" was so powerful and life-giving that it was said that they "turned the world upside down" (Acts 17:6). Christianity as "the Way" is dynamic and contagious. Christianity only as doctrine, religious attendance, and ministry performance is dull and often sterile.

Yet, it can be difficult to describe Christianity as "the Way" especially in the everyday places of life. It can feel somewhat like trying to follow a trail while hiking above tree line. Below the tree line, it is easy to follow a path cut into the soft ground between trees that have been marked to identify the trail. Above tree line, it is a different story entirely. There are no trees to bear trail markings and no worn down soil to reveal the trail. Because of this, it is difficult at times to even find, let alone follow the trail above tree line. Many hikers get lost, especially when storms blow in, diminishing sight, and increasing the difficulty of the journey. For this reason, generations of hikers that have gone before have built cairns above tree line as helpful markers to show the hikers that will follow the direction in which to travel.

For those who are unfamiliar with hiking or with cairns, a word of explanation is in order. Cairns are piles of stones that are placed by the trail. Some cairns are small, only made from a few stones neatly stacked like a snow man. Others are massive piles, containing hundreds of stones. Whether big or small, cairns of all forms have helped hikers stay on course for generations.

In this book, we will erect a cairn to guide us in the way of following Jesus. This cairn contains five "stones" that address five foundational questions every person must answer if he or she is to follow Jesus. These questions are:

— **What** are we to do as we follow Jesus?

— **How** are we to follow Jesus?

— **When** are we to follow Jesus?

— **With Whom** are we to follow Jesus?

— **Where** are we to follow Jesus?

It is our hope that this cairn will help you gain clarity as to what it looks like to follow Jesus in your day-to-day life. However, clarity of understanding isn't all we hope this book accomplishes, for clear thinking alone is not enough to cause us to follow Jesus, especially when the path becomes difficult. If we are to fully follow Jesus, the deepest longings of our hearts must find their fulfillment in Him. We have come to realize this truth through our own journey in discovering the Five Stones.

The building of the Five Stones way of life began when a group of pastors called the "Missional Architects" were gathered in 2009 to discuss the issue of church health within the Evangelical Free Church of America. This group was jokingly referred to as the "scary guys" since many of them were ministering in non-traditional churches whose methods, at times, raised questions. The common thread uniting this group of pastors was that everyone longed to see the church lovingly and effectively engaging our culture in a way that would lead to multitudes coming to follow Jesus. Over the subsequent three years as we prayed and discussed what steps the EFCA should take to carry out the mission of Jesus in our time, we found that our longings led to something much deeper. Our longings were for more of Jesus Himself— more of His presence, more of His power, which will inevitably lead to more of His mission.

We realized that this longing for more of Jesus would not be satisfied by gaining more biblical knowledge, increased church attendance, or additional ministry activity, as good as all those things are. We found that this longing can only be satisfied in a day-to-day way of life following Jesus. This led us to form the Five Stones as a cairn, defining the way of life in Christ that God was calling us to live. Though we were located in different places across the country, we agreed together to practice the Five Stones with our families.

This way of life profoundly affected all our families. First of all, the Five Stones deepened our families in Christ by giving us tangible practices by which to grow as followers of Jesus. It also led to increased mission. As a result of living the Five Stones, God sent two of the families to Berlin, Germany to develop this way of life in that pivotal city. He prompted another family to start a network of families equipped to make disciples in their neighborhoods in suburban Colorado. He directed another family to live out the Five Stones within a house church network in rural Colorado. He led two other families to work within the traditional church structure in New England to align families and churches to the Five Stones way of life.

As we practiced this way of life in our specific locations, God gave us opportunities to teach it to many others. There was interest especially in the Northeast, so we held a series of retreats in upstate New York and New Hampshire. Those who attended these retreats requested more resources to assist them in living and reproducing the Five Stones in their families, churches, and communities. This book is the answer to that request.

We must state that while we are trying to present a clear and compelling way of life in Christ, we are not claiming this is the only way to follow Jesus. There are as many different ways of following Jesus as there are styles of cups in our cupboards. There are formal wine glasses, plastic kiddy cups, coffee mugs, and water glasses, just to name a few. While these cups may look very different, they are all similar in that they are merely containers. A way of following Jesus, like a cup, is merely a container. Any truly Christian way must contain the living wine of Jesus Christ. He is the point within the way. He provides life. He nourishes. He satisfies. Yet while the wine of Christ is the point, a cup is necessary. Described in this resource is a cup which contains the wine of Christ. While it is not the only way, we believe the Five Stones is a really good way that is simple, adaptable, transferable, and captivating.

If you want to journey through life actively engaged in following Jesus rather than just knowing facts about Him, attending religious services, and performing ministry activities, then we invite you to join us in learning and living the Five Stones. As we learn to follow Jesus in the everyday, we will find in Him the true end for our longings. Following Him, we will experience the joy of His presence for which our hearts were made. As we walk in His presence, our eyes will be opened to the incredible greatness of His power for us who believe. As we live by His power, we will have the privilege of being part of His kingdom mission.

While the concept of the "Five Stones" may be new, the substance of this way of life is quite old. In this book we will describe simple yet powerful principles and practices that have guided faithful communities of Christ's followers down through the ages. We will use a lot of Scripture not as proof-texts, but to describe this way of following Jesus in a manner that will stir and captivate your heart. Unless otherwise noted, all Scripture will be quoted from the English Standard Version. We will also use stories from our own experience to illustrate the beauty and power of this way of following Jesus. It is our prayer that as this Five Stones way of life continues to expand, it will help many people to follow Jesus who is the Way, the Truth and the Life and then lead others to do the same.

Prologue

The Mountain and the Kingdom

"Come, let us go up to the mountain of the lord, to the house of the God of Jacob, that He might teach us His ways and that we may walk in His paths." Isaiah 2:3

Before we describe the different stones comprising the Five Stones way of life, we must describe the mountain up which this way of life is leading. If we do not start here, we run the risk of missing the whole point of the journey. The Five Stones are not the focus or goal of the Christian life any more than a cairn is the focus or goal of a hike. So, what mountain are the Five Stones leading us up? Consider these words from the prophet Isaiah:

> *It shall come to pass in the latter days*
> *that the mountain of the house of the Lord*

shall be established as the highest of the
        mountains,
    and shall be lifted up above the hills;
and all the nations shall flow to it,
    and many peoples shall come, and say:
"Come, let us go up to the mountain of the Lord,
    to the house of the God of Jacob,
that he may teach us his ways and that we may
walk in his paths."
For out of Zion shall go the law,
    and the word of the Lord from Jerusalem.
He shall judge between the nations,
    and shall decide disputes for many peoples;
and they shall beat their swords into plowshares,
    and their spears into pruning hooks;
nation shall not lift up sword against nation,
    neither shall they learn war anymore.
O house of Jacob,
    come, let us walk in the light of the Lord.
Isaiah 2:2-5

The mountain pictured in Isaiah's words is the whole point of the Fives Stones way of life. This mountain described by the prophet is nothing less than a picture of the Kingdom of God come to earth. If we are to grasp the purpose of the Five Stones, then we must understand the Kingdom of God.

The phrase "Kingdom of God" in the Scriptures is to be understood as the "rule of God." That is different than our modern usage where we most always use "kingdom" to mean the "realm over which a King rules." "Kingdom" in the Scriptures can refer to the realm over which a king rules, but primarily points to "the authority to rule" or "the sovereignty of a king."[1]

> *The Lord has established his throne in the*
> *heavens,*
> *and his kingdom rules over all.* Psalm 103:19

> *Your kingdom is an everlasting kingdom,*
> *and your dominion endures throughout*
> *all generations.* Psalm 145:13

While God's rule is everlasting, the realm over which He rules is not. This is what is wrong with our world. Though we all desire the benefits of God's rule over our world, we have all rejected His right to rule over our lives. Instead we attempt to run our own lives, on our own terms. The result of this rejection is not freedom, as we had hoped, but enslavement to the Kingdom of darkness. We find ourselves controlled by Satan, sin, and the fear of death.

In Isaiah 2, we see the wonderful promise that God will once again make all things right upon His Mountain. His Kingdom will be lifted up above the kingdoms of every other ruler. The nations will come to meet with Him and learn His ways. He will settle all disputes and end every conflict. Every human being longs for life on this mountain, where we will realize the fullness of the life that is only to be found in God's Kingdom. We all long for the establishment of real and lasting peace. We all cry out for suffering to end. We all yearn for death to be defeated. All of these longings are fulfilled on God's mountain. Let's listen to the words of the prophet Isaiah.

On this mountain the Lord of hosts will make for
    all peoples
a feast of rich food, a feast of well-aged wine,
of rich food full of marrow, of aged wine well
    refined.
And he will swallow up on this mountain the
    covering that is cast over all peoples,
    the veil that is spread over all nations.
    He will swallow up death forever;
and the Lord God will wipe away tears from all
    faces,
    and the reproach of his people he will take
    away from all the earth,
    for the Lord has spoken. Isaiah 25:6-8

THE KING AND HIS KINGDOM

The prophets promised that the life described in Isaiah 25:6-8 on God's mountain would be made available when God's Anointed King from the line of David arrived to rule (Isaiah 11:1-10). Under His rule, righteousness and peace would flourish. The enemies of God and His people would be defeated so that *"they shall not hurt or destroy in all my holy mountain."* (Isaiah 11:9)

This King's rule would not be temporary, but *"of the increase of his government and of peace there will be no end."* (Isaiah 9:7) Daniel also prophetically pointed to the future rule of God's anointed King when he interpreted one of King Nebuchadnezzar's dreams. In the dream, a stone struck and demolished a statue of a man. This statue was composed of various materials that Daniel interpreted to be different earthly kingdoms. The stone that struck the statue then *"became a great mountain that filled the whole earth."* Daniel said of the stone that became a great mountain: *"And in the days of those kings the God of heaven will set up a kingdom that shall never be destroyed, nor shall the kingdom be left to another people. It shall break in pieces all these kingdoms and bring them to an end, and it shall stand forever."* (Daniel 2:44) A King of God's own choosing would come and establish a righteous rule that would triumph over all other kingdoms and would fill the whole earth and endure forever.

When Jesus began His ministry, more than seven hundred years after the prophets spoke of "the mountain of the Lord" and the coming King, crowds of people flocked to Him. What was so stunning, compelling and confusing for the crowds was that Jesus quoted the Old Testament prophets and talked about the Kingdom of God as if He was the Anointed King and His Kingdom was at hand.

> *And he came to Nazareth, where he had been brought up. And as was his custom, he went to the synagogue on the Sabbath day, and he stood up to read. And the scroll of the prophet Isaiah was given to him. He unrolled the scroll and found the place where it was written,*
>
>> *"The Spirit of the Lord is upon me,*
>>   *because he has anointed me*
>>   *to proclaim good news to the poor.*
>> *He has sent me to proclaim liberty to the*
>>   *captives*

and recovering of sight to the blind,
to set at liberty those who are oppressed,
to proclaim the year of the Lord's favor."

And he rolled up the scroll and gave it back to the attendant and sat down. And the eyes of all in the synagogue were fixed on him. And he began to say to them, "Today this Scripture has been fulfilled in your hearing." Luke 4:16-21

"The time is fulfilled, and the kingdom of God is at hand…" Mark 1:15

He backed up these bold statements about Himself with demonstrations of power that revealed His authority to rule and the available blessings of His Kingdom to those who would receive Him.

"But if it is by the finger of God that I cast out demons, then the kingdom of God has come upon you." Luke 11:20

Jesus *IS* the Anointed King, the rightful ruler of all. Wind, waves, sickness, blindness, deafness, lameness, leprosy, and death itself must obey Him.

The Mystery of the Kingdom

As we read the Gospel narratives we see that people were obviously excited about the arrival of God's Kingdom, and many received His Kingdom like little children, full of trust and overjoyed with great delight. Others though, understandably scratched their heads and wondered, "How can the Kingdom of God be here when there is still so much suffering in the world?" Many today ask this very same question.

Jesus devoted much of His preaching to addressing the mystery of how the Kingdom of God was at hand while other kingdoms that opposed His rule still existed. Consider the following parable:

> *And he said, "With what can we compare the kingdom of God, or what parable shall we use for it? It is like a grain of mustard seed, which, when sown on the ground, is the smallest of all the seeds on earth, yet when it is sown it grows up and becomes larger than all the garden plants and puts out large branches, so that the birds of the air can make nests in its shade."* Mark 4:30-32

In this parable, and many others, Jesus reveals the mystery that the Kingdom of God is here, but in a way that is easily overlooked. The Kingdom of God is truly here among us, but has not yet come in its entirety. One day, the Kingdom of God will be unmistakable, filling the whole earth. But for now, we can experience in seed form the blessings of the Kingdom, such as His presence, His power, His mission.

The Gospel of the Kingdom

Jesus not only explained the nature of God's Kingdom during this age, but He also invited people to receive the Gospel of the Kingdom.

"The time is fulfilled and the Kingdom of God is at hand; repent and believe in the gospel."
Mark 1:15

Most people who have been Christians for some time assume they understand what the word "Gospel" means. So as we read the words of Mark 1:15 we assume we know what Jesus meant when he proclaimed the "Gospel." But our modern understanding of "Gospel" and Jesus' intended usage of "Gospel" are not the same thing.

First of all, the word "Gospel" in Jesus' day was not a religious word, but a political word concerning a "proclamation of victory." In 490 BC there was a famous battle fought between Greece and Persia called the Battle of Marathon. Greece won a decisive victory at the Battle of Marathon and legend has it that a Greek soldier ran with the news of victory from Marathon to Athens which was a distance of just over 26 miles. The Greek word for this news was *"euangelion,"* translated as "Gospel," which means the good news of victory.[2] Because this victory had been won, the people of Athens were safe and could enjoy peace and freedom in their kingdom. The "Gospel" was about the victory the King had accomplished and was good news to those who lived under His rule.

In contrast, the Gospel today quite often has little to do with the rule of a King. Instead it is treated more like an insurance policy to avoid justly deserved punishment for sin within the context of eternity. This pseudo-Gospel often revolves around human beings making a business deal with God that serves their own self-interest, rather than Jesus the King reclaiming humanity so that it might become His own treasured possession. The heartbreaking result of this human-centered gospel is people who have some form of belief in Christ but have little experience of life in His Kingdom.

Though Jesus' proclamation of the Gospel of the Kingdom includes salvation of individual human beings, it is intended to be much more. It is the announcement that He is the Anointed King who has come to establish God's Kingdom on earth as it is in Heaven. His Kingdom is available to humanity now and is advancing in the realm of this world. One day, He will return in glory to remove all opposition and establish His Kingdom forever.

> *"The kingdom of the world has become the kingdom of our Lord and of his Christ, and he shall reign forever and ever."* Revelation 11:15

The Means of Victory

To understand the Gospel, we must not only grasp the fact that Jesus is the rightful and victorious Ruler of all, but also the means by which He has won the victory. It was expected by most of the Jews in Jesus' era that the promised Kingdom that Isaiah pictured as "the mountain of the Lord" would come about by the violent bloodshed and overthrow of God's enemies. Their expectation was that the Anointed King promised by God would arrive in power and crush all earthly opposition underneath his feet. But had Jesus won victory through military conquest, we would not have been able to enter the Kingdom of

God because we don't have the requirements necessary for entrance. Let's reflect on the words of King David:

Who shall ascend the hill of the LORD?
  And who shall stand in his holy place?
He who has clean hands and a pure heart,
  who does not lift up his soul to what is false
  and does not swear deceitfully.
He will receive blessing from the LORD and
  righteousness from the God of his salvation.
Psalm 24:3-6

An honest self-assessment for all of us reveals that our walk is not blameless and our hearts are deeply conflicted. Had Jesus won victory through military conquest, we would not have been able to enter the Kingdom of God. No invitation from God would be offered to us so that we might "Come to the Mountain of God to learn my ways and walk my paths." Instead, we would have heard "don't touch the mountain, lest you die" just as the Israelites heard when Moses was preparing to meet with God on Mt. Sinai to receive the Law.

However, there is no King like Jesus. He was not preoccupied with his own comfort and safety. Instead, He chose the path of humility and sacrifice. Though He deserved to dwell on the "holy hill" referred to in Psalm 24, He chose to descend that hill into the dark valley where humanity dwelled so that He might journey up the hill of Calvary to rescue us. Upon that hill, Jesus, the Anointed King, accomplished the victory— not by crushing His enemies and shedding their blood, but by being crushed Himself and shedding His own blood. Amazingly, this had been God's plan all along:

> But it was the Lord's good plan to crush him and
> cause him grief.
> Yet when his life is made an offering for sin,
> he will have many descendants.
> He will enjoy a long life,
> and the Lord's good plan will prosper in his
> hands.
> When he sees all that is accomplished by his
> anguish,
> he will be satisfied.
> And because of his experience,
> my righteous servant will make it possible
> for many to be counted righteous,
> for he will bear all their sins.
> I will give him the honors of a victorious soldier,
> because he exposed himself to death.
> He was counted among the rebels.
> He bore the sins of many and interceded for
> rebels. Isaiah 53:10-12 NLT

The Good News is that Jesus has won the victory in a way that allows "rebels" to enter His Kingdom. In His death, the sin that makes us rebels is dealt with. Sin's power is broken. Sin's penalty is erased. In His resurrection, Jesus' eternal life is given to us. His righteousness is now ours. We are now invited to ascend the hill of the Lord because we have been given the clean hands and pure heart that only belong to Jesus. God's Kingdom that will ultimately fill the earth forever is available now and we can enter it by faith in Jesus!

The Call of the Kingdom:
Receive the Kingdom

Jesus invites us to travel up the Mountain of Calvary in order to enter the Kingdom of God. In His Kingdom we will experience the blessings of learning His ways and walking in His paths. But how are we to come and journey upon the mountain of the Lord?

Jesus said that the Kingdom of God must be received. *"Truly, I say to you, whoever does not receive the kingdom of God like a child shall not enter it."* (Luke 18:17) Jesus was quite clear that we receive His rule and become His followers in His Kingdom through repentance and belief. "The time promised by God has come at last!" he announced. *"The time is fulfilled, and the kingdom of God is at hand; repent and believe in the gospel."* (Mark 1:15)

Repentance is a turning, a change of mind that leads to a change of behavior. We must change our mind about who is in charge. Sin occurs when we put anyone or anything other than God in the place of God in our lives. We must repent and believe in Jesus, our Savior and Lord.

We need to recognize that our modern use of the word "belief" hinders our understanding of Jesus' teaching. We think of belief primarily as knowledge, "facts we know to be true but may or may not impact our lives." For instance, you may believe that George Washington was the first President of the United States. That fact is true, but does little to shape your life. The concept of "belief" in the Bible means far more than intellectual agreement to a statement of truth. To believe is to **rely** upon that which you have believed in. So, to repent of your sin and rely upon the Gospel is to trust in Jesus' victory for our lives now and forever.

Walk in the Kingdom

An initial reception of Jesus' Kingdom, while good and necessary, is not all there is to following Jesus on the Mountain of God. Far from it! The Apostle Paul tells us once you've received Jesus as Lord and entered His Kingdom, there's a whole hike ahead. *"Therefore, as you received Christ Jesus the Lord, so walk in him."* (Colossians 2:6)

Many professing Christians stop on the trail and stand there wondering why they don't experience much of Jesus' Kingdom. They enjoy little of the freedom he claims to offer, little of the peace that he says is ours, and little of the power needed for mission. The reality is that there aren't many scenic views from a trailhead. The beautiful vistas come further on in the journey. Jesus is looking to lead us further up the path toward glory, if we will but only follow.

The Five Stones are all about guiding us further up on the path of Jesus. While this journey is wonderful, it is not easy. The path is filled with danger, difficulty, and detours. Therefore, Jesus said it is wise to consider the costs of the journey before we set out so that we don't find ourselves unprepared when the going gets rough. John Bunyan's classic, Pilgrim's Progress describes well the difficulty in the journey of following Jesus.

> *Christian and Formalist and Hypocrisy all went on till they came to the foot of an Hill, at the bottom of which was a Spring. There was also in the same*

place two other ways besides that which came straight from the Gate; one turned to the left hand, and the other to the right, at the bottom of the hill: but the narrow way lay right up the Hill, and the name of the going up the side of the Hill, is called Difficulty. Christian now went to the Spring and drank thereof to refresh himself, and then began to go up the Hill...

The other two also came to the foot of the Hill. But when they saw that the Hill was steep and high, and that there was two other ways to go; and supposing also that these two ways might meet again, with that up which Christian went, on the other side of the Hill: Therefore they were resolved to go in those ways; now the name of one of those ways was Danger, and the name of the other Destruction. So the one took the way which is called Danger, which led him into a great Wood; and the other took directly up the way to Destruction, which led him into a wide field full of dark Mountains, where he stumbled and rose no more."[3]

As we follow Him in this broken yet beautiful world, we must take up our own cross, endure suffering, and experience hardship. The reason we are called to walk the path of difficulty is that in the midst of hardship we find the path of true life. We were made for life on the mountain! We were saved to walk with Jesus and experience the glorious sights and breathtaking wonders found only as we scale the heights of His Mountain. Let the words of Hebrews 12 spark your imagination and stir up your heart to worship our King.

You have not come to a physical mountain, to a place of flaming fire, darkness, gloom, and whirlwind, as the Israelites did at Mount Sinai. For they heard an awesome trumpet blast and a voice so terrible that they begged God to stop speaking. They staggered back under God's command: "If even an animal touches the mountain, it must be stoned to death." Moses himself was so frightened at the sight that he said, "I am terrified and trembling."

No, you have come to Mount Zion, to the city of the living God, the heavenly Jerusalem, and to countless thousands of angels in a joyful gathering. You have come to the assembly of God's firstborn children, whose names are written in heaven. You have come to God himself, who is the judge over all things. You have come to the spirits of the righteous ones in heaven who have now been made perfect. You have come to Jesus, the one who mediates the new covenant between God and people, and to the sprinkled blood, which speaks of forgiveness instead of crying out for vengeance like the blood of Abel.

Be careful that you do not refuse to listen to the One who is speaking. For if the people of Israel did not escape when they refused to listen to Moses, the earthly messenger, we will certainly not escape if we reject the One who speaks to us from heaven! When God spoke from Mount Sinai his voice shook the earth, but now he makes another promise: "Once again I will shake not only the earth but the heavens also." This means that all of creation will be shaken and removed, so that only unshakable things will remain.

Since we are receiving a Kingdom that is unshakable, let us be thankful and please God by worshipping him with holy fear and awe. For our God is a devouring fire. Hebrews 12:18-29 NLT

The author of Hebrews compels us to consider both the dangers and the glories that we will experience in this journey of faith. If we do not realize the dangers, we may grow naive and walk unprepared.

When I was a teenager, a man from my hometown lost his life while hiking late in the summer on Mt Washington, the highest peak in the White Mountains of New Hampshire. The weather was fair when he began the four mile hike to the summit, but once he got above tree line, a freak snowstorm blew in. He hadn't expected life-threatening weather, so he only packed a thin windbreaker which was no match for harsh weather he encountered. Unfortunately, his story of heartache and loss is one among many stories of hikers who died on Mt Washington as a result of being unaware as to how dangerous a journey it can be. —*Sam*

It is important that we recognize there are life and death perils in the journey of faith as well. We must heed the voice of our Guide and give ourselves completely to following Him.

While the author of Hebrews is honest about the perils of the journey, he doesn't focus there only. He also motivates us onward by stirring our hearts to anticipate the glory of the mountain. Journeying on the mountain of the Lord, we experience the joy of festive celebration along with the hosts of heaven, the fellowship of God's holy children, the unshakeable destiny of God's Kingdom, and the presence of God Himself— the One for whom we ultimately long. This is not only a future reward, but a present reality as we experience Jesus in our lives.

Jesus has made it possible for us to journey up the Mountain of the Lord. The Five Stones will serve as markers for our path. We invite you to walk with us. In the words of C.S. Lewis, "Come further up, come further in."[4]

Reflection

What part has "the Kingdom of God" played in your understanding of the Gospel?

In what ways is the Kingdom of God foundational for following Jesus?

What about the Kingdom of God do you find challenging? What questions do you have?

Chapter 1

STONE ONE

Love God, Love Others, and Make Disciples

What Are We to Do as We Follow Jesus?

But when the Pharisees heard that he had silenced the Sadducees, they gathered together. And one of them, a lawyer, asked him a question to test him. "Teacher, which is the great commandment in the Law?" And he said to him, "You shall love the Lord your God with all your heart and with all your soul and with all your mind. This is the great and first commandment. And a second is like it: You shall love your neighbor as yourself. On these two commandments depend all the Law and the Prophets." Matthew 22:34-40

Walking with Jesus in the Kingdom of God is about learning to live His way of life. This way of life can be summarized into three interconnected strands that Tom Johnston and Mike Chong Perkinson call the "Irreducible Core" (IC) of the Christian faith. Together they make up the substance of Stone One: *Love God, Love Others, and Make Disciples.*[5]

These three strands are referred to as the "Irreducible Core" because together they form the core DNA of the Christian way of life. You can do more than these three things and be following Jesus, but you can't do LESS than these three things and be following Jesus. This first stone becomes the foundation upon which the entire Five Stones Way of Life is built.

This "Irreducible Core" comes from two of the most famous passages of Scripture, commonly referred to as the Great Commandment (Matthew 22:34-40) and the Great Commission (Matthew 28:18-20). In this chapter, we will first consider what it looks like to love God and love others. These two aspects of the IC are the heart of the Christian life because they are the eternal, unchanging values of God's Kingdom. "Make Disciples" is part of following Jesus in this present age, because we live in a world that is not yet filled with the values of God's Kingdom. But one day soon, the Mountain of God will fill the whole earth. Loving God and loving others will be the universal norm. But as that time has not yet come, we must teach people to learn God's ways and walk His paths. We will explore how we go about making disciples in the second part of this chapter.

THE HEART OF THE KINGDOM:
Loving God and Loving Others

The Heart of God's Kingdom is love because the heart of God is love. God exists in a perfect community of love— Father, Son, and Holy Spirit. We have been created to share in this love. Jesus helps us to understand this life of love in His teaching of The Great Commandment to an expert in religious law. Jesus' teaching completely surprised the law expert who had asked Jesus "which of the commandments is the most important." Jesus' answer was surprising for a couple reasons. First, He moved the conversation from a discussion about rules to a conversation about relationships. Jesus was essentially telling the lawyer that life in God's Kingdom wasn't about getting the rules right but rather living within right relationships. Jesus boldly stated that the whole of the Old Testament could be summarized into a call to live rightly in a relationship with God and relationships with others. Everything in the Old Testament depended on those two relationships.

The shift from rules to relationships was surprising for the lawyer, but even more so was the fact that Jesus said that those two relationships were inseparable. We can't have right relationship with God without having right relationships with other human beings. Love for God is the vertical expression of living in the Kingdom. Love for others is the horizontal expression of living in the Kingdom. At the intersections of those two relational expressions, we find the beating heart of Kingdom life.

Most people connect with the idea of life being all about love, but what do we mean when we talk about God's love? In Jesus' statements to the lawyer, He gives definition to the kind of love that we are to practice. He says that we are to love the Lord with *all our heart, soul, and mind.* Jesus is saying that we are not to love God in a compartmentalized fashion but with the totality of our being. We don't usually think of love in this holistic manner. We chop up our lives into compartments with love for God being one among many. This leads to the compartmentalization that we so often see among Christians who "love" God with songs of praise in a church gathering, but fail to "love" him with their finances, their calendar, their relationships. Jesus completely rejects this notion by simply saying *"If you love me, you will keep my commandments."* (John 14:15) Our loving allegiance to King Jesus therefore shows itself in every aspect of our lives!

Loving God is not so much about religious acts of worship, but about living in a devoted relationship of trust. This is why love for God naturally flows into love for others. If we lack love for others, we expose our lack of love for the One we call our God. What surprised the lawyer was not so much Jesus' statement about loving God, but that he linked it to loving others. Jesus was saying that we cannot truly love God apart from loving people as well. Jesus' disciple John also taught this:

> If anyone says, "I love God," and hates his brother, he is a liar; for he who does not love his brother whom he has seen cannot love God whom he has not seen. And this commandment we have from him: whoever loves God must also love his brother.
> 1 John 4:20-21

In Luke's account of the Great Commandment, the lawyer pressed Jesus further regarding the command to love and received an answer in a story.

> And behold, a lawyer stood up to put him to the test, saying, "Teacher, what shall I do to inherit eternal life?" He said to him, "What is written in the Law? How do you read it?" And he answered, "You shall love the Lord your God with all your heart and with all your soul and with all your strength and with all your mind, and your neighbor as yourself." And he said to him, "You have answered correctly; do this, and you will live." But he, desiring to justify himself, said to Jesus, "And who is my neighbor?" Jesus replied, "A man was going down from Jerusalem to Jericho, and he fell among robbers, who stripped him and beat him and departed, leaving him half dead. Now by chance a priest was going down that road, and when he saw him he passed by on the other side. So likewise a Levite, when he came to the place and saw him, passed by on the other side. But a Samaritan, as he journeyed, came to where he was, and when he saw him, he had compassion. He went to him and bound up his wounds, pouring on oil and wine. Then he set him on his own animal and brought him to an inn and took care of him. And the next day he took out two denarii and gave them to the innkeeper, saying, 'Take care of him, and whatever more you spend, I will repay you when I come back. ' Which of these three, do you think, proved to be a neighbor to the man who fell among the robbers?" He said, "The

one who showed him mercy." And Jesus said to him, "You go, and do likewise."
Luke 10:25-37

Jesus' story made it clear that God intends us to love others whom we would otherwise avoid. He intends us to love people in sacrificial, tangible ways, as we would desire to be loved. He intends for love to fulfill law. Based on his reading of the law, the lawyer would not have thought that God intended him to touch impure, unclean, or ungodly people. But amazingly, there is no one who is on God's "untouchable" list. We see this kind of love lived by followers of Jesus who are caring for the homeless, adopting children with disabilities, ministering to the sick, and visiting those in prison. God's love compels His people to love others with His love.

> I was given the opportunity to show the love of Jesus to Kat, a young poverty stricken women who lived in the ghetto in a major city in New England. Kat had experienced a very difficult life as a child and as a result of this trauma, battled with an incredibly negative self image. Kat had been terribly abused by those who had called themselves "Christians" in her past, but was able to move beyond those difficulties so that my wife Maria and I could become an ongoing and positive part of her life. Both Maria and I felt that even though we had little in common with Kat, God's Spirit desired us to share our love and our family with her. The first time we visited with her in the north end of her city, none of us felt safe. Her apartment had no appliances and

contained the tell tale tracks of cockroaches, yet she fashioned us a meal and made us feel welcome in the home she shared with a large number of her other family members. Though Kat did not know Jesus personally, we did. It was clearly our calling to bring the hope of the Kingdom to bear in her life, and so we did. The experience was a difficult one, fraught with frustration and disappointments, yet we are trusting that the Gospel seeds we have scattered will one day take root. —*Foye*

The Jesus way of life is to be lived at the intersection of vertical love for God and horizontal love for others. To truly love others, we must draw our love from God; and to truly love God we must demonstrate His love to others. We cannot enjoy one without experiencing the other. This is why we will demonstrate the Five Stones way of life through use of both vertical and horizontal practices as we continue our journey in building the cairn throughout the remaining pages of this book.

The Wonder and Dilemma of the "New Command" to Love

Jesus summed up all of the Old Testament's teaching with these two interdependent relationships. Yet Jesus did not come to rehearse or reiterate Old Testament moral laws and tell us to try harder. He came to love us as we haven't loved Him, and in doing so, enable us to love others as we have been loved by our incredibly merciful, unfathomably gracious God.

Jesus is the ultimate "Good Samaritan." He loved God and loved others as we should, but haven't. Unlike the priest and Levite, Jesus didn't see His relationship with God as reason to avoid us as we lay in our sinful and broken condition along the gutters of life's highway. Instead, His close relationship with His Father compelled Him to cross the gulf separating God and humanity. Jesus went out of His way and humbly inconvenienced Himself in order to love us. And His love was not mere sentiment; it was "hands on" and came at incredible cost. He cared for our sorrows not by wishing us well, but by making our sorrows His own. He healed our wounds not by applying a superficial bandage, but by becoming wounded Himself. He paid for our sin not with two denarii, but with his own blood. *"By this we know love, that he laid down his life for us..."*. (1 John 3:16)

When we receive Jesus' love into our lives, it heals, transforms, and compels us to love even as we have been loved. That is why Jesus was able to say to His disciples *"A new commandment I give to you, that you love one another: just as I have loved you, you also are to love one another."* (John 13:34) What was new was not the commandment to love, but the ability to keep the commandment and actually love! As we trust how loved we are by God, His love through us becomes *"supernaturally natural, an organic expression of His life lived in us."*[6]

How are we "established in God's love"

We cannot emphasize enough that our love for God and others is to be a response to the love we have already received from God. The fact that God loved us prior to, and apart from, any good we have done runs completely counter to the prevailing mindset of our performance oriented culture. It says we must perform well in order to receive love, but that is not how it works with God. Consider the narrative of Jesus' baptism found in Mark 1:9-11. As Jesus came up from the waters of the Jordan River, the Spirit descended on Him in the form of a dove and the Father spoke these beautiful words of affirmation: *"You are my beloved Son; with you I am well pleased."* At this point in Jesus' life, He hadn't done any miracles or preaching. The Father's approval was not based on what Jesus had DONE, but who Jesus IS. Jesus' relationship of love with His Father was foundational for Him. He loved and ministered FROM a place of love and approval, not FOR love or approval.

The wonder of the Gospel, is that we can love and minister from the same source of love and approval as Jesus. When we place our faith in Jesus, God not only forgives our sin, but adopts us into His family as His sons and daughters. We don't become employees in God's business but His cherished children. We aren't like the fairy tale Cinderella either, who was part the family but made to be second class, living on the periphery, constantly demeaned. In John 17:23 we read that the Father loves his adopted children as much as He loves His Son, Jesus. Therefore, the Father's words said at Jesus' baptism are said to us as well if we are "in Christ": "You are my much loved son or daughter; and I am very pleased with you." God loves us and is pleased with us, not because of what we have done or will do, but because of who we are in Christ. We are His children and God loves His kids passionately. Wow! This fact is absolutely life changing.

God has given both of our families a window into the depth of His love for His adopted children through our own experiences of adoption. Foye and Maria adopted their son, Zayden in 2009 and Sam and Wendy adopted their oldest daughter, Nadia in 2007. We adopted our children, not because they behaved well or did anything to earn a place in our family. We adopted them out of the overflow of God's love as we have experienced it in our family. Once adopted, Zayden & Nadia's behavior behavior didn't ensure their continued place in our family or our continued love. As a matter of fact, despite what everyone thinks, life is far from perfect once an adopted child comes home. Years of being unable to trust authority figures do not magically melt away. Lack of trust almost always results in self-protective behaviors like lying, stealing, and defiance. The only thing that can build trust when it has been lost is steadfast love.

Becoming grounded in God's love as His cherished children is transformational. We are freed to love people who don't love us, because we aren't dependent on receiving love from them in return. We draw love from God. We don't try to measure up or prove anything to God. Jesus has already measured up for us. We are sons and daughters of the Most High God; princes and princesses of the Kingdom. When we believe who we truly are, it changes how we live. Remember this incredible truth, *what you do flows from who you are!*

Remember who you are

Most of our failure to love well comes from a failure to believe or remember who we truly are. One epic story that has captured the imagination of both our families over the past several years is Andrew Peterson's "The Wingfeather Saga."[6] It is the story of a family who though royalty, live ordinary lives as ordinary people in an out of the way village far from their homeland, a homeland which has been overrun by a ruthless & diabolical enemy. The people they live among have mixed reactions once their true identity is revealed. Some villagers disbelieve and scoff while others befriend. The Wingfeather children themselves struggle to believe and live according to their true identity. But everyday, when the mother, Nia, sends the three kids to school, she tells them as they leave, "Remember who you are." We love that! She doesn't say, "Be good" or "Behave" or "Others are watching." Those statements, so common among Christians, can be attempts to motivate right behavior through guilt. Nia's instructions were a daily grace reminder of their true identity. She had established a daily practice that helped her family remember who they were so they would not base their self worth or their relationships on the acceptance and approval of others.

We all need regular practices to remind us of who are if we are going to follow Jesus in loving God and others. Without tangible practices, we have a Christian philosophy with a lot of knowledge, but not a Christian way of life full of love. Therefore, practices are essential to following Jesus.

A large part of hiking is the practice of seemingly mundane walking that eventually leads to glorious mountaintop views.

> Every summer my son and I spend a couple days "man camping." This usually involves a hike of some sort. Early on in the hike questions like "are we there yet" or "how much longer" usually come up. It takes hours of trudging along in the woods, putting one foot in front of the other, before we get above tree line to see the glory of the view. —*Sam*

Much of following Jesus is also about seemingly mundane "spiritual practices" that lead us to glory. A spiritual practice is something that we do to walk with God and learn His ways. By regularly engaging in spiritual practices, we train so that we are able to walk with Jesus higher up and further on the mountain. As we go, we find that we are able to love in ways that we were previously unable because we have "trained" in Jesus' way of life.

For each stone, we are going to present two practices that enable us to live the principles we are teaching. The practices are described in vertical and horizontal terms. The vertical practices shape our love for God. The horizontal practices shape our love for others.

Now, we are going to describe two practices that can help us live the principles of Stone One. These practices may seem mundane, inconvenient, or may even turn you off completely. That's okay with us. We aren't saying you have to adopt them exactly as we have practiced them. You may do something different altogether. However, permit us to share a little advice in the form of story:

> One day a lady criticized D. L. Moody for his methods of evangelism in attempting to win people to the Lord. Moody's reply was "I agree with you. I don't like the way I do it either. Tell me, how do you do it?" The lady replied, "I don't do it." Moody retorted, "Then I like my way of doing it better than your way of not doing it."[7]

These practices are by no means the only ways to grow in love for God and others. We know of other ways that followers of Jesus practice these two core principles. Our question to you is, "what is your practice for loving God and loving others?" If you don't have a tangible practice, then we encourage you to put the following two into practice.

VERTICAL PRACTICE:
Connect at a heart level with the Lord through the Scriptures.

The Bible anchors us in the knowledge that God loves us regardless of our performance. The Bible is also the primary doorway through which we experience the source of love— the Father, Son, and Holy Spirit. We must allow the Bible to capture our hearts and form our thinking about who God is and who God says we are. If we don't allow the Bible to do this, something else will! As we prayerfully read the Scriptures, we are reminded of God's steadfast love for His children. We are then able to receive His love afresh and respond to His love with trusting obedience.

Therefore, we encourage you to select a daily Scripture reading plan. You can find a number of ideas at *youversion.com, rbc.com,* or *biblegateway.com.* Use the following steps as a guide for connecting at a heart level with the Lord through the Scriptures.

1. **Quiet your heart**
   Tell God what you are thinking and feeling. Ask Him to speak to you and reveal His heart.

2. **Listen for what God is saying**
   Read through the passage slowly (maybe even a couple times). As you read, listen for a word, phrase, or idea that "stands out to you" in an especially meaningful way.

3. **Reflect on what God is saying**
   What is God impressing upon your heart? Is it something He is telling you about Himself? About what He wants you to do? Why do you think He is saying this to you today?

4. **Respond to what God is saying**
   Praise Him for what He reveals about Himself, confess the areas of sin that are graciously brought to the light. Thank Him for His goodness in cleansing. Cast your burdens on Him. Ask God to act in your life in specific ways that cause His Kingdom to come and will be done on earth as it is in heaven.

As you practice this, remember that reading Scripture is not an end unto itself. For too many Christians, that is exactly what it becomes. We are tempted to evaluate our Christian walk based on the frequency and depth of Scripture reading. Consider Jesus' words to the religious leaders of His day *"You search the Scriptures because you think that in them you have eternal life; and it is they that bear witness about me, yet you refuse to come to me that you may have life."* (John 5:39-40) We read the written Word to lead us to the Living Word who will lead us to live His way of life.

Reading the Bible is not the only way that the truths of the Bible shape us. As a matter of fact, if we don't find other mediums for interacting with the Scriptures, our faith can remain at a "head" level without descending to the heart. Singing the truths of Scriptures and reading Scripture saturated stories are two great ways that our hearts, as well as our minds, become connected to the God of the Scriptures. Another way the Scriptures can penetrate our hearts is through the reciting of daily affirmations. The Huggard and Belyea families recite the following affirmations to daily anchor their hearts in God's truth revealed in His Word.

Affirmations

Love God (Matthew 22:34-40)
We are children of God. We exist to be loved by God with everything He is and to love Him with everything we are.

Love others as you love yourself
(Matthew 22:34-40)
We are servants. We will love others with the love of Christ, seeking their welfare before our own.

Make disciples, as you go (Matthew 28:18-20)
We are stewards of the Gospel. We are sent by Jesus to make more and better disciples for Him everywhere we go.

Be creative in developing your own way of connecting at a heart level with the Lord through the Scriptures. Talk to other followers of Jesus and ask them about their practices for reading the Scriptures. Ask also about how other mediums such as music, art, or story have shaped their hearts with truths of Scripture. As you let the Scriptures saturate your mind and heart, you will be like the tree described in Psalm 1, which is planted by streams of water and bears fruit in due season.

HORIZONTAL PRACTICE:
Connect at heart level with one another

God's love is designed to flow outward in tangible ways into our relationships with others. One of the most helpful ways to express love for others is found in learning to listen to another's heart. A great tool for learning to communicate at a heart level is the practice of SASHET. This is an acronym for the six dominant emotions that we typically feel: Sad, Angry, Scared, Happy, Excited, and Tender. When we listen to the condition of a friend's heart and then share the condition of our own heart with them, something powerful, connective and redemptive occurs. This type of heart sharing is foreign to most people because we tend to communicate at a safe, surface level that keeps us from truly knowing and loving one another.

How then does SASHET work? One person will "check in" by describing the emotion(s) they are experiencing at that moment and the reason(s) why. After the person shares their heart's emotional state and reasons that are contributing to it, the listener has the opportunity to respond in the following appropriate way. "This is what I heard you say. How can I minister to you now? Did you simply want to share what was on your heart, would you like prayer, or are you seeking to receive counsel?" This question allows the one who has shared to direct the ministry function that follows. It may be that the listener may be asked to offer intercessory prayer (presenting the needs of the one who has just shared unto God) or engage in a time of listening prayer (waiting quietly upon the Holy Spirit to provide a word of encouragement for the one who has just shared their heart).

> Sam and I are prayer partners. We share our hearts together regularly. We pray for one another, asking God's Spirit to give us words of encouragement, affirmation and hope for one another. One of the recurring themes that comes up as we share our hearts together is God's call for us to rest in Him. He sees what we are doing. He delights in our love for him. He exults in our commitment to advancing his Kingdom, yet he persistently calls us to rest. Many of the words, phrases, songs, and pictures

the Lord has given us have revolved around faithfulness in the face of adversity. As I, Foye, look back over my prayer journal, I see innumerable occasions where Jesus has moved me to encourage my brother to move forward in the face of personal adversity. SASHET has given us a great resource for sharing our hearts with one another in a way that helps to pray for one another, listening to God's encouraging words. —*Foye*

Some people use SASHET to connect around the dinner table with their family and friends. They take turns "checking in" as they share a meal together. Some people share naturally, whereas others have to be drawn tactfully and tenderly with a few low-key follow up questions such as: "Tell us a little more about that" or "What do you think is causing you to feel like that?" Sometimes SASHET triggers a time of simple sharing and listening. At other times it leads to a time of prayer for one another at the close of the meal. Regardless of how SASHET unfolds, it creates space for natural, unscripted and non-coercive communication; communication which knits our hearts together as we live on mission together with our King.

We also use SASHET in church small groups and retreat settings to help people learn to connect at a heart level. By giving people a structured way to identify and share their current emotional state, it helps people connect in ways they previously were not able. We frequently see people express great surprise at the real encouragement they receive by transparently sharing within the context of gracious listening, sometimes with people they didn't know before the meeting began.

It is important to recognize that for SASHET to be effective, gracious listening is necessary. SASHET is not the time for counsel or instruction. This is very challenging for many people to learn. It seems that we by nature are quick to offer a solution or a spiritual pat answer when someone shares a difficulty.

We remember leading a group in which a wife shared that she was feeling sad and anxious about the current season of life for her family. As soon as she finished, her husband jumped in and tried to put a "happy face" on the story by highlighting how God could use this season for good. While his words were true, the effect on his wife was negative. We could see her wither as he spoke because he was attempting to fix her perspective and emotional state rather than simply be with her in it. We don't like pain or tension, so we try to relieve it as quick as possible, but God uses the pain and tension to accomplish His purposes in us. Intimacy grows as we share each others burdens.

Loving God and loving others are the core values of life in God's Kingdom. Therefore, the practices of connecting at a heart level with God through the Scriptures and connecting at a heart level with one another are core to our way of life. These practices can be tweaked and adapted to fit your life situation, but in some form these practices must be present if you are going to follow Jesus in the the Five Stones way of life.

MAKE DISCIPLES

Now that we have explored the first two strands of Stone One, "loving God and loving others", we need to explain the third strand that comprises this stone: "make disciples." We find the call to make disciples in Jesus' final instructions to His disciples before He ascended to the Father.

> *Now the eleven disciples went to Galilee, to the mountain to which Jesus had directed them. And when they saw him they worshiped him, but some doubted. And Jesus came and said to them, "All authority in heaven and on earth has been given to me. Go therefore and make disciples of all nations, baptizing them in the name of the Father and of the Son and of the Holy Spirit, teaching them to observe all that I have commanded you. And behold, I am with you always, to the end of the age."* Matthew 28:16-20

Before ascending to the Father, Jesus gave His disciples the Great Commission which forms the third part of the Irreducible Core. The Great Commission is the natural outflow of the Great Commandment. Those who truly love God and love His Image in others desire to see His gracious Kingdom come and His good will done on earth as it is in heaven. Therefore, to be a follower of Jesus, we must not only give ourselves to loving God and loving others, but also give ourselves to making disciples.

Before we teach what the Great Commission is all about, let's first note the historical and geographical setting in which it originally took place. Jesus directed His disciples to a mountain in Galilee to receive His final instructions. As we look through the Biblical narrative, we see that mountains are the setting for a massive number of major events in the course of redemptive history. (That's fancy theological language for the unfolding of God's great rescue plan!) Noah's boat came to rest upon Mount Ararat. Abraham sacrificed a ram God provided instead of his son on a mountain in Moriah. The law was given to Moses on Mount Sinai. Jesus taught His most famous sermon on a mountain. Jesus revealed His glory in His transfiguration on a mountain. Jesus was crucified on Mount Calvary. Jesus ascended from the Mount of Olives. Mountains are frequently the setting for God's saving activity.

It is deeply intriguing to consider the mountainside setting in light of the Kingdom mission Jesus was about to give. Remember, the "mountain of the Lord" that will fill the earth is the Old Testament picture of God's Kingdom filling the whole world. The prophets also spoke of God's desire for His people to be messengers who shout the good news of His Kingdom from the mountain tops.

O Zion, messenger of good news,
   shout from the mountaintops!
Shout it louder, O Jerusalem.
   Shout, and do not be afraid.
Tell the towns of Judah,
   "Your God is coming!"
Yes, the Sovereign LORD is coming in power.
   He will rule with a powerful arm.
See, he brings his reward with him as he comes.
   He will feed his flock like a shepherd.
He will carry the lambs in his arms,

holding them close to his heart.
He will gently lead the mother sheep with
their young. Isaiah 40:9-11 NLT

Jesus called his disciples together on a mountain to instruct them in how they were to go about filling the world with the Gospel of the Kingdom until the day when He would return and establish His Kingdom in its fullness.

What is the vision of the Great Commission?

Whenever we speak of the Great Commission, we usually go directly to vs. 19 *"Go therefore and make disciples..."* Instead we should first observe the vision for the Great Commission that is found earlier in vs. 18 *"All authority in heaven and on earth has been given to me."* In saying this, Jesus is announcing that He has won the right to completely rule over both heaven and earth. He is the victorious King who has conquered the spiritual forces of darkness and reclaimed ownership of everything for His Kingdom. He accomplished this victory when He *"disarmed the powers and authorities, he made a public spectacle of them, triumphing over them by the cross."* (Colossians 2:15) Jesus ruling is Good News for all creation, including humanity (Colossians 1:20-22). All things are being set right and will one day be made good as new when *"the kingdom of the world has become the Kingdom of our Lord and his Christ."* (Revelation 11:15)

When we are captivated with the vision of the earth filled with the Kingdom of God we are able to engage in the Great Commission with confidence and enthusiasm. Confidence comes from the knowledge that Jesus has already won the victory and His Kingdom will never end. Enthusiasm flows from our participation in the triumphal procession of Jesus' Kingdom as He reconciles all things to Himself.

What is the mission of the Great Commission?

In light of the vision of Jesus ruling, what then is our mission? How will Jesus' Kingdom advance in this age before His return? It is first important to recognize how Jesus said His rule does NOT advance in this age. Jesus' disciples inquired before His ascension *"Lord, will you at this time restore the Kingdom to Israel?"* Since Jesus had already "proclaimed the year of the Lord's favor," they now expected Him to bring "the day of God's vengeance" (Luke 4:18-29 & Isaiah 63:1-2). But Jesus does something completely unexpected. Rather than taking vengeance on His enemies, He offers us reconciliation. Jesus refuses to send His followers out with swords, but instead sends them out with the Gospel of Peace. In this age, Jesus is not advancing His Kingdom by overthrowing all other kingdoms, but subverting them as He captures the hearts and lives of those enslaved by the rule of darkness.

Jesus' mission for advancing His Kingdom on earth is clearly spelled out in verse 19 *"Go therefore and make disciples of all nations..."* "Make disciples" is the imperative; it is the mission. Everything else in the statement is descriptive of how to go about the mission. Our focus for the rest of this chapter is understanding how we are to go about the task of making disciples.

What is a disciple?

Jesus lived and ministered within the ancient near-eastern Jewish culture in which it was common for a young man to seek out a rabbi and ask to become his disciple. If accepted, this young disciple would re-orient his life to take on his rabbi's "yoke," which was the rabbi's interpretation of Torah and resulting way of life. The disciple would be eager to learn what the rabbi knew, do what the rabbi did and ultimately, to become like the rabbi. Quite simply, a disciple is a learner of a rabbi's way of life.

Jesus, unlike the other rabbis, sought out His disciples and invited them to follow Him. This invitation to become a disciple was first and foremost an invitation to relationship. The disciples joined Jesus in His life. They went with him to weddings, funerals, and dinner parties. To Jesus, discipleship was not an impersonal series of meetings for the purpose of communicating doctrinal information. Discipleship was the process of transmitting His way of life to his friends as they walked through life together. Life was the curriculum, relationship was the classroom, and Jesus' "yoke" was the content.

There was good reason to become Jesus' disciple. His "yoke" differed from all the other rabbis. Their interpretation of Torah was harsh and demanding. Jesus compassionately invited people, *"Come to me, all who labor and are heavy laden, and I will give you rest. Take my yoke upon you, and learn from me, for I am gentle and lowly in heart, and you will find rest for your souls. For my yoke is easy, and my burden is light."* (Matthew 11:28-30) As we accept Jesus' yoke and learn His way of life, we find rest for our weary souls.

What then is Jesus' yoke? We've already explored it in the first part of the chapter. It is the Great commandment to Love God and Love Others. Jesus summed up the totality of Torah with those two commands. Discipleship to Jesus meant accepting the "yoke" of the Great Commandment and learning to live according to it. This is why Jesus told his disciples, *"just as I have loved you, you also are to love one another. By this all people will know that you are my disciples, if you have love for one another."* (John 13:34-35) Jesus taught them His way of life by living it with them. They in turn are to live it with others. As they live it, everyone will recognize that they have become like their rabbi.

This point is especially well illustrated in Acts 4:13. For those of you unfamiliar with this passage, the scene opens with Peter and John being tried by the high priest, elders, rulers, and other key religious gatekeepers for preaching the Gospel in the Temple Courts. Listen carefully to verse thirteen, *"Now when they saw the boldness of Peter and John, and perceived that they were uneducated, common men, they were astonished. And they recognized that they had been with Jesus."* These first disciples, though uneducated commoners, resembled their Rabbi, they sounded like him, they shared His convictions and His priorities. They had assumed His yoke completely and would not be dissuaded from sharing its life-giving truth even when threatened with persecution.

The goal of discipleship for Jesus' followers in every age is the same. By learning His way of life, we become like Him. In becoming like Him, His Kingdom is realized in an ever greater measure. Tom Johnston ably emphasizes this goal of Jesus' yoke by saying, "the Kingdom of God lived out in the context of two 'Great Relationships' is the central core of the yoke of Jesus. The main outcome of His educational process was to lead people out into the transcendent, transforming, holistic realization of God's loving Kingdom rule."[8]

Disciples of Jesus learn His way of life so that they become like Him. Disciples of Jesus also learn His way of life *so that they can teach others to become like Him.* They are to become the "rabbis." Jesus was upfront about His plans when He first called His disciples: *"Follow me, and I will make you become fishers of men."* (Mark 1:17) Jesus was doing with his disciples what they were to in turn do with others.

Jesus intends that every person who becomes a disciple of His be made into a "fisher of men." That sounds intimidating, especially given the brokenness of our lives. But Jesus didn't say that we were to make ourselves into teachers of His way of life. He said "I will make you..." Jesus does the making. Colossians 1:16 says about Jesus, *"For by him all things were created, in heaven and on earth, visible and invisible, whether thrones or dominions or rulers or authorities—all things were created through him and for him."* Jesus is the Maker of all and He excels at what He does. What he wants is for us to be made into His masterpieces of grace that will draw others into the beauty of His story (Ephesians 2:10). Our task is to follow

Him. He does the making and He does it well. So, whatever your situation, believe that Jesus can use you and will make other disciples through you.

How do we make disciples?
Live all of life with the intention to make disciples

Thankfully, Jesus does not give us the task of making disciples without instructing us how to go about it. His first instruction directly precedes the command to make disciples— "*Go.*" The word "Go" is not a command in the Greek, the ancient language in which the New Testament was originally written. Therefore, there is some difficulty translating it appropriately into English. It could be translated, "going" or "as you go." Either way we realize that Jesus is sending His disciples from that point forward to live their lives with the intention to make disciples.

"Go" is not just for missionaries who travel to another country or paid professionals within a church structure. Every disciple is to live with the intention to make disciples "as they go" about their lives. Every facet of a disciple's life is to become a disciple-making opportunity. Isn't that encouraging and empowering? Jesus desires to use you in the midst of your every day life to shape the eternal destiny of others.

Whether we are going to work, to school, out with friends, we are to go with Jesus' Kingdom purpose of making disciples. *"And whatever you do, in word or deed, do everything in the name of the Lord Jesus, giving thanks to God the Father through him."* (Colossians 3:17)

Immerse people into the person, presence, and life of God

The second aspect of discipling-making appears in the phrase *"baptizing them in the name of the Father and of the Son and of the Holy Spirit."* New disciples are to be baptized, which means "to immerse," into the "name" (singular) of the "Father, Son, and Holy Spirit" (plural). In the Scriptures, "the Name of the Lord" is synony-mous with the Lord himself. *"The name of the Lord is a strong tower; the righteous man runs into it and is safe."* (Proverbs 18:10) So we see that Jesus intends new disci-ples to be immersed into God Himself— His Person, His Presence, and His Life.

This instruction has rightly led us to the practice of water baptism which is the public demonstration of a new disci-ple's identification with the Person, Presence, and Life of Jesus. While affirming the significance of water baptism, we also want to suggest that there is prior baptism that must happen if a disciple is to be truly immersed in the life of Christ.

On Pentecost, just ten days later, the disciples were them-selves immersed into the person, presence and life of God and "clothed with power from on high" when the Holy Spirit came and in-dwelt them. They immediately began fulfilling Jesus' disciple-making mission by inviting others to *"Repent and be baptized every one of you in the name of Jesus Christ for the forgiveness of your sins, and you will receive the gift of the Holy Spirit."* (Acts 2:38)

What every disciple desperately needs is to be immersed into God, for it is not possible to "observe all that Jesus commanded" apart from being filled with the Spirit of God. Yet this is so often what happens. Ian Thomas refers to this kind of discipleship as "evangelical house training" where disciples try to conform to Jesus' teaching through behavioral modification instead of being led by the power that makes obedience possible. The result of "evangelical house training" is droves of frustrated Christians that know the message of Jesus but are unable to live the life of Jesus. So, the question is, how are we to "immerse people into the person, presence, and life of God so that disciples can be connected with the power to enable them to live the way of Jesus?"

Making disciples through baptism involves a process that begins with **incarnation**. We can begin to immerse people into The Person, Presence, and Life of God through life on life relationship. Jesus, the Word, became flesh and "moved into the neighborhood." He made God known through His life on earth lived in relationship with those to whom He was sent. The Spirit of God indwells Jesus' followers so that in a similar but lesser way, God's person, presence, and life can be revealed through us as well. People must encounter not just the message of Jesus but the life of Jesus in His people if they are to become mature disciples.

Incarnation is essential to immersing people into God, but much more is needed. There must be the impartation of spiritual life through **conversion**. *"Jesus answered, "Truly, truly, I say to you, unless one is born of water and the Spirit, he cannot enter the kingdom of God. That which is born of the flesh is flesh, and that which is born of the Spirit is spirit. Do not marvel that I said to you, 'You must be born* *again.'"* (John 3:5-7) Like Jesus and Peter at Pentecost, we must invite people to repent of their sin and and receive the Spirit of God. It is right and good that water baptism accompany this step of conversion.

Yet still another aspect is needed if a disciple is to live immersed in the Person, Presence, and Life of God. The New Testament Scripture counsels us to be **"filled** with the Spirit."** Though every believer in Jesus has the Spirit of God living within them, not every believer is living by the direction of the Spirit. As followers of Jesus, we must learn how to yield all aspects of our lives to the Spirit's control so that our lives demonstrate the values of the Kingdom. Only by the Spirit's power can we live the Christian life.

Teach people HOW to do what Jesus taught

Jesus instructed his disciples to make disciples by *"teaching them to observe all that I have commanded you."* Theologian Dallas Willard, when commenting on this portion of Scripture refers to the contemporary evangelical church's lack of intentional disciple-making as the "great omission from the great commission." We frequently omit this last crucial emphasis, not because we are lazy (though that may occasionally be a factor) but because we don't understand Jesus' method of teaching. We commonly think "teaching" is the passing on of information in a classroom setting, such as preaching or discipleship class. But teaching for Jesus was not reduced to a once a week classroom-styled lecture. Jesus taught His disciples by investing years of relationship in which He revealed His way of life through word and deed. The Apostle Paul also discipled people in this manner. He instructed people to *"imitate me as I imitate Christ."* To Timothy, he said: *"You, however, know all about my teaching, **my way of life...**"* (2 Timothy 3:10 NLT) The inconvenient truth for our modern corporate church structures is that disciples aren't mass produced through curriculum dispensed over the course of weeks; they are hand crafted in relationship invested over the course of years.

If we are to take seriously Jesus' call to teach people to observe all that He commanded, then we must open up our homes and lives to those who God is calling us to disciple. Like Paul, we must be able to say *"Because we loved you so much, we were delighted to share with you not only the gospel of God but our lives as well."* (1 Thessalonians 2:8 NLT) Disciples need to be shown how to live Jesus' way of life in their marriages, families, workplaces, schools, etc— not just told to do it from a preacher's pulpit or a teacher's podium. For instance, a sermon series or DVD curriculum may be able to explain the principles of Christian marriage, but experiencing how a Christian marriage operates over dinner with another follower of Jesus shows the principles at work in real life. We are designed by God as relational beings. We need to be taught Jesus' way of life through ongoing relationship.

We must be authentic and humble, not perfect or skilled.

Every follower of Jesus is to be involved in making disciples. Recognizing just how important this task is to the advance of our Lord's Kingdom can often leave people feeling inadequate or overwhelmed. You may lament how little you know of Jesus' way of life or how imperfectly you follow what you do know. Allow us to let you in on a little secret— that's true of every follower of Jesus, even his original disciples. Look at what the verses preceding the Great Commission say of Jesus' disciples: *"when they saw him they worshiped him, but some doubted."* These men were not superhuman pillars of faith, instead they were ordinary, flawed human beings whom Jesus loved dearly and planned to use for His glory. Even after they received this great commission and the empowering Holy Spirit, they still messed up sometimes. Yet God mysteriously worked through both the good and bad of their lives in a way that revealed His mercy and grace. Even the Apostle Paul who wrote most of the New Testament letters and planted many of the first churches said this about himself: *"Christ Jesus came into the world to save sinners"—and I am the worst of them all. But God had mercy on me so that Christ Jesus could use me as a prime example of his great patience with even the worst sinners. Then others will realize that they, too, can believe in him and receive eternal life."* (1 Timothy 1:15-16 NLT)

Jesus seems to make a habit of using the humble, not the perfect. Consider the woman at the well who had been divorced five times and was living with another man at the time of her encounter with Jesus (John 4:1-45). Look at the tortured wild man who had been demon possessed and lived naked in a cemetery (Mark 5:1-20). Neither person had the credentials to qualify with most mission boards. Yet, both became Kingdom emissaries of mercy and grace that God used mightily.

Satan's name means "accuser" and that is precisely what he does. He tries to convince us that we are unfit for the King's service by accusing us of sin and inadequacy. His accusations are frequently effective because the material he draws from is true. He simply points to our sin and our weaknesses. While that part is true, what follows is nothing but lies. He whispers that because of our sin and weakness God doesn't love us, doesn't want good things for us, and isn't able to use us. Therefore, he tempts us to hide our sin and weakness behind a charade of delusional self-righteousness. If we buy into this temptation, we will do one of two things— either fake it or check out. Acquiescing to either option advances the evil one's scheme. He either lures us into hypocrisy that ends up discrediting the Kingdom or sidelining us from Kingdom work because of our pain.

Jesus does not want us to live enmeshed in hypocrisy or sitting out on the far end of the bench. Instead, He calls us to expose our sin and weakness so that His healing light may shine on them. Confessing our sin short circuits the power of Satan's accusation. We can say, "It is true, I have sinned, but there is no condemnation for me in Christ Jesus. Sin is no longer what is truest about me. In Christ, I am holy, blameless, and without fault." These confessions lead us to a greater awareness of God's mercy and grace which then spills over into a greater ability to live according to His ways. Confessing sin not only benefits us as disciples of Jesus, but is part of making disciples of others for it models how Christians deal with sin in light of our true identities.

We should not only confess sin but also admit weakness. Weaknesses are imperfections in our bodies and personalities that are not sinful, just undesirable.

> I have a slight speech impediment that causes me to stutter at times in conversation. I hate it. In my estimation it keeps me from effectively discipling others. But I have discovered that the opposite is true. A man in my church once approached me and told me that he loved that I have a speech impediment because he felt closer to me as a man with weaknesses rather than a slick professional without any. —*Sam*

Satan would have us think that only the strong, beautiful, skilled, or popular can be effective in making disciples. But God's plan for making disciples isn't to use only polished celebrities, but to work through ordinary people who in comparison seem "foolish, weak, and low" (1 Corinthians 1:27-31). We agree with the words of Paul: "*For what we proclaim is not ourselves, but Jesus Christ as Lord, with ourselves as your servants for Jesus' sake. For God, who said, "Let light shine out of darkness," has shone in our hearts to give the light of the knowledge of the glory of God in the face of Jesus Christ. But we have this treasure in jars of clay, to show that the surpassing power belongs to God and not to us.*" (2 Corinthians 4:5-7)

Jesus is the King of kings who is now increasing His Kingdom on the realm of earth through the disciple making work of His followers. As C.S. Lewis said, "*the Church exists for nothing else but to draw men into Christ, to make them little Christs. If they are not doing that, all the cathedrals, clergy, missions, sermons, even the Bible itself, are simply a waste of time. God became Man for no other purpose. It is even doubtful, you know, whether the whole universe was created for any other purpose.*"[10] One day, Jesus will return and this disciple-making work will be done, but until then we are extended the privilege of living our normal lives with the overarching intention of making disciples of Jesus.

PRACTICES

Since making disciples is about helping others learn to live Jesus' way of life, all of the Five Stones practices are involved in making disciples. As you learn the practices that shape this way of life, you simply come alongside others and help them learn to live the way you are living. A good place to start are the vertical and horizontal practices from earlier in this chapter for loving God and loving others. Consider who God has placed in your life with whom you can engage in both of those practices. It may be your family, a co-worker, or a neighbor. As you help them learn to connect at a heart level with God through the Scriptures and connect at a heart level with one another through SASHET, you are helping that person learn what it means to be a citizen in God's Kingdom, following Jesus' way of life.

Reflection

Without using Biblical language, write down how you honestly think God feels about you. After doing so, compare your answer with these Scriptures: Ephesians 1:3-14 and Romans 8:14-17.

How are you experiencing God's love currently?

In what relationships do you need God's love to flow more fully through you? What would that look like? Consider the link between God's love and your ability to love in the relationships you listed as your read 1 John 4:7-21.

Reflect upon & describe your own discipleship process. Who has taken the time to disciple you? How have they done so?

Whom is God calling you to invest in and begin discipling?

How can you disciple others using the principles and practices of Stone One?

Chapter 2

STONE TWO

The Leadership of the Holy Spirit

How Do We Follow Jesus?

"I am with you always, to the end of the age..."
Matthew 28:20

When Jesus first called his disciples to follow Him, there wasn't a whole lot of confusion as to what He meant. His disciples literally dropped what they were doing and followed Him as He traveled from town to town. Jesus was the leader; they were the followers. He taught; they learned. He sent; they went. What was confusing for the disciples is how He would continue to be with them and lead them after He left them and returned to the Father. In John's account of Good Friday, the disciples' confusion about Jesus' imminent departure is so obvious it nearly leaps off the page. They didn't comprehend what He meant about

leaving and they didn't want Him to go. As was His practice, Jesus' went on to reassure them of His good intentions without revealing the full scope of His plan.

> *"Nevertheless, I tell you the truth: it is to your ad-*
> *vantage that I go away, for if I do not go away, the*
> *Helper will not come to you. But if I go, I will send*
> *him to you"* John 16:7

It seemed inconceivable to Jesus' first disciples (and to
many of His disciples today) that it was better for Him to
leave the earth and return to heaven. How could it get any
better than having Jesus, the promised King in flesh, leading them in His Kingdom life and mission? The thought
was impossible to fathom, much less process. Yet Jesus
knew that his physical departure from this earth would not
mean abandoning His disciples to their own efforts to live
out His Kingdom life. His departure was instead intended
for the purpose of drawing even closer to them.

> *"I will not leave you as orphans; I will come to you.*
> *Yet a little while and the world will see me no more,*
> *but you will see me. Because I live, you also will live.*
> *In that day you will know that I am in my Father, and*
> *you in me, and I in you."* John 14:18-20

The "Helper" Jesus promised is the Holy Spirit who would
fill Jesus' disciples with His presence. Jesus considered the
Holy Spirit to be so important that He told His disciples not
to go about His mission after His ascension, but to *"stay*
in the city until you are clothed with power from on high."
(Luke 24:49) On Pentecost, ten days after Jesus returned
to The Father, He fulfilled His promise to His disciples and

the promise made to the Old Testament faithful centuries earlier. God "poured out His Spirit" into the lives of Jesus' disciples so that they were filled with Jesus' presence and power. This was the necessary next step in the advance of God's Kingdom on earth. Paul said that this is the mystery that was hidden for ages, but now revealed: God's plan is to dwell WITHIN His people— making them His body so that through them He might fill all in all (Colossians 1:27 & Ephesians 1:23).

Jesus' disciples today actually have it better than the Old Testament heroes of faith and even the first disciples who walked the dusty roads of Judea with Him. We have Jesus' Spirit within us wherever we go so that we are never separated from His loving presence. *"God's love has been poured into our hearts through the Holy Spirit that has been given to us."* (Romans 5:5) We have God at work within us giving us the ability to obey Him *"for it is God who works in you, both to will and to work for his good pleasure."* (Philippians 2:13) We have God's power to fulfill Jesus' mission. *"But you will receive power when the Holy Spirit has come upon you, and you will be my witnesses in Jerusalem and in all Judea and Samaria, and to the ends of the earth."* (Acts 1:8) We believe that Jesus was right; it was for the best that He went away, that we might be closer to Him than before.

Following Jesus now is about learning to allow the Holy Spirit, who is the Spirit of Jesus, lead our lives, families, and churches. We cannot follow Jesus without the Holy Spirit's daily guidance and empowerment. Our attempts to live the Christian life apart from a daily, personal submission to the Holy Spirit sets us up for feelings of frustration, discouragement and inadequacy. Lack of purposeful cultivation of intimate contact with the Holy Spirit results in powerlessness, purposelessness, and all too often, ministry failure. Therefore, it is essential that every disciple develop a full understanding of who the Holy Spirit is and learn how to experience Him personally so that we may walk closely with Jesus and carry out His Kingdom mission today.

Following Jesus is about following a person not just principles. We need a guide, not just a map for this journey. We are not saying that following Jesus doesn't involve following the teachings of Jesus revealed in Scripture; it does involve that, and much more. We need the person of Jesus to direct us in the application of His principles to the specific situations of our everyday lives. We need the person of Jesus to empower us to live according to His teachings since we lack the ability to do so otherwise. We need the person of Jesus to fill our hearts with his love, grace, and peace. In his devotional book, *The Indwelling Life of Christ*, Sir Ian Thomas summed up the need to follow the person of Jesus quite well:

> *To be entirely honest, I know of nothing quite so boring as Christianity without Christ. Countless people have given up going to a place of worship simply because they are sick of going through the motions of a dead religion. They are sick of trying to start a car on an empty tank. What a pity that there are not more people around to show them that Jesus Christ is alive...The utmost need in every ministry group, every missionary outreach, every denomination, is to rediscover the Lord Jesus*

Christ and the indispensability of His indwelling presence within the believer. This means encountering the risen living Lord who shares His life with us on earth on our way to heaven...so that He may accomplish through us what He began to do in His own physical body two thousand years ago...The Christian life is nothing less than the life He lived then...lived now by Him in you.[11] - Sir Ian Thomas

Jesus intends to lead His followers today through the indwelling presence of His Holy Spirit. But how do we follow the leadership of the Holy Spirit?

Walking by the Spirit requires listening!

It doesn't take a rocket scientist to figure out that listening is a really important part of any healthy relationship. If one person in a friendship, marriage, or business partnership rarely listens to the other, that relationship is destined for problems. Our relationship with Jesus also requires listening. Jesus told His original disciples that He would have more to say to them after His departure.

"I still have many things to say to you, but you cannot bear them now. When the Spirit of truth comes, he will guide you into all the truth, for he will not speak on his own authority, but whatever he hears he will speak, and he will declare to you the things that are to come. He will glorify me, for he will take what is mine and declare it to you. All that the

Father has is mine; therefore I said that he will take
what is mine and declare it to you."
John 16:12-15

Notice in the prior verses from the Gospel of John that
Jesus shares with his disciples that though they have
learned much from him, there is much more he wants
them to know. This further explanation of the Father's
purposes and the process whereby the Son desires his
servants to carry out these purposes will be revealed by
the Holy Spirit. So, through the Holy Spirit, Jesus is speaking to His disciples today. The question is, "are we are
listening?" The point of the very famous passage found
in Revelation 3:20-22 is that Christians are called to listen
for their Lord, not the more commonly preached evange-
listic application intended to convince unbelievers to "ask
Jesus into their hearts."

"Behold, I stand at the door and knock. If anyone
hears my voice and opens the door, I will come in
to him and eat with him, and he with me... He who
has an ear, let him hear what the Spirit says to the
churches." Revelation 3:20-22

The Spirit of God speaks to us through the Scriptures, in
the midst of our prayers and through the testimony of other believers, but it is possible to ignore Jesus by failing
to listen to the Holy Spirit. This is why the Apostle Paul
warned us:

Do not quench the Spirit. Do not despise proph-
ecies, but test everything; hold fast what is good.
1 Thessalonians 5:19-21

Notice in these verses above that the Spirit of God can be not only resisted but also quenched. To quench something means to extinguish or put out. We who have been baptized by the Spirit upon our conversion need to yield to the Spirit's continuing operation in our lives or we will find ourselves causing the fire of God which is intended to burn brightly within us to be diminished significantly, sometimes even to the point of being nearly put out.

How then do we quench the Spirit by our activities? Though we may quench the Spirit by willingly entertaining sin and engaging in activity that grieves the heart of God, this passage from 1 Thessalonians helps us to understand that we can resist the works of God by despising prophecies that are spoken over and into our lives.

We both believe that prophecy has a continuing role in the church today and that we need to carefully and prayerfully obey that which the Holy Spirit seeks to speak into to our hearts. We agree with respected evangelical Bible scholar and professor Dr. Wayne Grudem when he says;

> *Although several definitions have been given for the gift of prophecy, a fresh examination of the New Testament teaching on this gift will show that it should be defined not as "predicting the future" nor as "proclaiming a word from the Lord" nor as "powerful preaching" but rather as "telling something that God has spontaneously brought to mind.*[12]

While it is not our intent to discuss the full range of Biblical teaching on prophecy, we submit to you that this instruction from Paul to the church at Thessalonica teaches us that disciples are called to carefully test and weigh that which they believe has been disclosed to them by the Holy Spirit in prayer or through another believer.

According to the Apostle Paul the purpose of God speaking His prophetic words through other people is for the the purpose of strengthening, encouraging, and comforting others (1 Corinthians 14:3). We test and weigh what we believe the Spirit may have given by measuring these words, thoughts or actions against what the Bible clearly teaches. We also measure it against our past experiences of God's faithfulness as it has been expressed in our lives. Is this message in keeping with God's character? Is it encouraging, strengthening, uplifting? Does this thought, idea or directive make much of Jesus and advance his kingdom? If so, it is quite probably from the Lord and is intended for to obey so that the Kingdom is advanced.

Often times, we in evangelical churches can doubt this voice and turn a deaf ear to its direction because we are afraid of being viewed as erratic, strange, or overly mystical. We have found that many times people in our churches have had experiences where they have felt promptings or leadings to do certain things such as make an unscheduled stop, or an unplanned telephone call. When we have obeyed these promptings or leadings, God has revealed how He was working at the same time in the lives of others who needed to hear a kind word, receive a visit, know that someone was praying for them, or even recognize that God had a specific word of encouragement He wanted relayed to them.

This idea is expressed clearly in the commentary on the Evangelical Free Church's Statement of Faith

> *The Spirit can guide us in practical ways by a mysterious inward prompting, which is spiritually discerned, or, more commonly, by simply leading us into godly wisdom through an understanding of the Word of God.*[13]

These promptings and leadings are the Holy Spirit communicating the Father's direction to us. It is the Lord crying out for us to seek His face, His will, His plan for our day rather than our coming to Him asking him to bless that which we have structured without even asking Him what His plans for us, our families and our churches may be.

> Early one morning during prayer I felt moved to pray for my friendBen and his family. This was unusual in that I hadn't seen Ben nor any member of his family in quite some time. The feeling was powerful, urgent, and unescapable. After praying for Ben, his wife, their daughter Bianca and the whole extended family; I felt compelled to call Ben and let him know that the Holy Spirit had called me to pray for him and his family that morning. I dialed his cell phone number and he answered on the first ring. After I identified myself, Ben asked if I had heard the news. Having no idea what he was talking about I said, "What news?" He then told me that his daughter Bianca's husband had just died of a massive heart attack and that Bianca was actually in the operating room as we were speaking having open heart surgery to repair a genetic abnormality

that her doctors had just discovered. My friend and his family were in turmoil and needed prayer support. It was the Holy Spirit who intruded that morning and directed me to pray, connect and then subsequently minister to this dear family. —Foye

HOW THEN DO WE HEAR FROM GOD?

Though not all of us hear from our Lord in the same way, all of us can indeed discern the voice of our Shepherd. We believe it is the birthright of every believer to hear the voice of God.

It took Maria and I a long time to get pregnant after we were married. We suffered through several courses of fertility medication and all of the subsequent side effects before we received the good news. We were going to have a baby! We found out it was going to be a girl and watched as maria's belly grew with each week that passed. One of the things Maria convinced me to do during the second trimester was to "talk into the tummy." This involved speaking to our child through the side of Maria's abdominal wall. We would then observe the whole child shift in utero towards the direction of my voice. I would then run around the bed, talk into the other side and watch the baby move towards my voice yet again. Several months later, Emilie was born after a very difficult delivery. She was bright red and screaming. Maria, though exhausted, whispered to me, "talk to her Foye" I called out

Emilie's name and welcomed the wee lass to our family. As soon as the baby heard my voice, the crying stopped and she struggled to turn her head toward the direction of my voice. The nurse who was attending us said, "she recognizes your voice daddy." That was an incredible moment for me. My child had recognized my voice and wanted to be where I was. —*Foye*

We are told in the Scriptures that all who trust in Jesus are born again, by the Spirit, into God's family. Our Father desires that we turn our face to Him and listen to His words of love and direction. Does the idea that your Heavenly Father is speaking to you and that you can recognize His voice sound far fetched? Listen carefully to what Jesus is saying to us in these incredible words found in John's gospel.

> "...He who enters by the door is the shepherd of the sheep. To him the gatekeeper opens. The sheep hear his voice, and he calls his own sheep by name and leads them out. When he has brought out all his own, he goes before them, and the sheep follow him, for they know his voice. A stranger they will not follow, but they will flee from him, for they do not know the voice of strangers...the Good Shepherd lays down his life for the Sheep..."
> John 10:2-5

We must be led out by the voice of the Good Shepherd

In order to follow Jesus, we must first be *led out* by His voice. The story of the Bible is that all of us have gone our own way and become ensnared by the evil one who seeks to steal, kill and destroy. We see this in the beginning of the Biblical story with Adam and Eve. They listened to the tempting voice of the evil one and strayed from God's path for their life. As a result, they (and every human being since) became enslaved, shackled by sin. In this place of captivity, we are like prisoners of war subject to noise torture. He constantly bombards us with words of temptation that proclaim the delights of sin. Then he hounds us with words of shame after we give in to temptation. The enemy shouts that our hardship is a sign from God that He doesn't love us. While we are held captive, we are deaf to the Good Shepherd's tender voice. We need to be set free from the noise of the evil one and given the ability to hear God's voice. Jesus has come for that purpose. He is the Good Shepherd who speaks tenderly and powerfully to His sheep to lead them out of captivity. As Charles Wesley wrote, "He speaks and listening to His voice, new life the dead receive."

> We adopted Zayden knowing that he had been profoundly deaf since birth. He received cochlear implants at around eighteen months old, just before we met him for the first time. These surgical procedures placed electronic hardware under the skin of his skull and within his ear canal. He was also given special sound processors which are worn like hearing aids externally. These processors, when

connected, provide a range of sound that rivals that of a hearing person. Without the processors, he can't hear a jet engine beside him. Without the processors he can't hear my voice, no matter how loud I speak. One day, science will be able to address his deafness. Until then we will go through the daily ritual of putting on his processors. Every time I put them on him I am reminded that apart from God giving me the ability to hear his voice I would be deaf to His call of love for me. —*Foye*

What does Jesus say that is so powerful that it overcomes the noise of the evil one and our own deaf ears? Hebrews 12:24 tells us that Jesus' blood speaks God's freeing word. Jesus, the Good Shepherd, didn't remain at a safe distance calling out to His captive sheep to come out to Him. No, He entered into our captivity and led us out by laying down His own life and becoming the sacrificial lamb. What shepherd would do that? The evil one can shout as loud as he wants trying to convince us that God's heart isn't good, that going our own way is better, that we are shameful sinners who God is eager to punish; but Jesus' blood speaks louder yet. It cries out that we have a truly *GOOD* Shepherd who is so good that he bled and died for us. It cries out that sin is fully paid for and forgiven. It cries out that nothing can separate us from God's love. Jesus is speaking to us today in the message of his sacrifice to lead us out of captivity and also to silence the noise of the enemy that we might hear God's voice.

We must follow the voice of the Shepherd

Jesus not only speaks to his followers to lead them out of captivity, but also to lead them along the path of freedom. *"he goes before them, and the sheep follow him, for they know his voice."* We see in the Scriptures how Jesus continued to go before and lead His followers even after his ascension: *"And when they had come up to Mysia, they attempted to go into Bithynia, but the Spirit of Jesus did not allow them."* (Acts 16:7) These first followers of Jesus were led not only by the principles of Jesus' teachings, but by real time instructions from Him about what they were to do. We must also expect that the Good Shepherd will speak to us through His Holy Spirit so that He might direct us in how we are to live everyday.

Below is a list of ways compiled by our friend and colleague Arthur Ellison that can help us to grow in discerning the voice of Holy Spirit.

We can hear the Holy Spirit speak to us through the Bible.

Though God speaks in many ways, the Bible is unique among all other means of divine communication because it is "the foundation upon which all acts of hearing are grounded, the criterion through which all such acts are to be judged and the guide by which all such acts are to be appropriated."[14] The Scriptures are foundational for hearing from God since they are not subject to the failings of human imagination or interpretation in the same way as other means of hearing from the Lord. The apostle Peter testified that the Scriptures have been given to us by the Holy Spirit *"no prophecy of Scripture comes from someone's own interpretation. For no prophecy was ever produced by the will of man, but men spoke from God as they were carried along by the Holy Spirit."* (2 Peter 1:20-21) Paul declared that *"all Scripture is breathed out by God."* (2 Timothy 3:16)

The Bible is foundational, yet as AW Tozer reminds us, it is not an end in itself.

> *Sound Bible exposition is an imperative must in the Church of the Living God. Without it no church can be a New Testament church in any strict meaning of that term. But exposition may be carried on in such a way as to leave the hearers devoid of any true spiritual nourishment whatever. For it is not mere words that nourish the soul, but God Himself, and unless and until the hearers find God in personal experience they are not the better for having heard the truth. The Bible is not an end in itself, but a means to bring men to an intimate and satisfying knowledge of God, that they may enter into Him, that they may delight in His Presence, may taste and know the inner sweetness of the very God Himself in the core and center of their hearts.*[15]

The Holy Spirit filled the authors of Scripture with the presence of Christ as they wrote and the Holy Spirit makes the Scriptures come alive today as readers are drawn into the very same Presence. The Spirit becomes, in effect, our teacher and interpreter. This gracious operation of the Holy Spirit is especially life-giving to those who previously read the Bible only as literature, a book whose words were to be critiqued and deconstruct- ed. However, once the Spirit grants illumination and new life, the words of God jump off the page and intersect our lives in beautifully disturbing and encouraging ways.

> One of the guys that I have the privilege of discipling is a younger man named Liam. Liam is a tough guy who, though growing up in the Catholic church, never had time for the Bible. He found it hard to understand, difficult to relate to, and irrelevant to the life he was living as a combat decorated Marine Corp veteran and New York City Policeman. One day after an elderly lady invited him to church, Liam gave his life to the resurrected Liamt. Suddenly the Bible came alive to him in ways that he had never experienced before. Liam found himself caught up in its majesty and power. He just couldn't put it down. He was so enthralled with its truth that he read it cover to cover in just under three months. When asked what has made the difference for him, he gives the credit completely to the illumining work of the Holy Spirit in his conversion. "What was once irrelevant has now become essential. I love how God shows me truth from His love letter to me. I will never be the same again." —*Foye*

We can hear the Spirit of God speak through a still small voice

Many people refer to this as a God given thought. Numbers of us who have walked with Jesus over the course of years remember occasions when we suddenly entertain a thought which is completely unassociated with what we were currently doing. This thought is often directional in nature. We have learned to heed these thoughts as they often reveal a mid-course correction that the Spirit of God is bringing to mind so as to align us with a current need that the Father wants us to address.

> *And after the earthquake a fire, but the Lord was not in the fire. And after the fire the sound of a low whisper.* 1 Kings 19:12

We can hear the voice of the Holy Spirit speak to us through the counsel of other disciples.

One of the greatest gifts Master Jesus has granted us in our Gospel inheritance is the family of believers. Many of them have walked with him for large parts of their lives and they can resource us with wells of hard won biblical wisdom that we have not yet accessed personally. The Spirit of God uses these older, more mature believers to be the vehicle through whom he verifies our identity, identifies our giftings, and provides divine counsel that will serve as confirmation of what we are hearing in our personal times of unhurried devotion.

We can hear the Spirit of God speak to us individually by seeing mental pictures while we are praying.

Just as the Lord sanctifies our souls, so too he sanctifies our imaginations. Often times we can be disturbed in our prayer process by seeing a picture that seems only tangentially associated with whatever we are praying about. Rather than being a distraction, they can indeed be the Spirit of God providing us with guidance and in effect, helping us to hear His voice more clearly.

We can hear the Spirit of God speak by knowing something with certainty.

This particular way of hearing from God results in a sense that "you just know that you know something with certainty." There is a conviction here that is granted by the Spirit so that we might obey and be used by the Father to be the conduit of his grace is someone's life.

We can hear the Spirit of God speak to us in seasons of prayer as we are moved with empathy for another.

Have you ever had that happen to you? You have arranged your office, bedroom, or living room to best facilitate prayer...for yourself, when suddenly, another person's name or face appears or is impressed upon you. You find yourself overcome with emotion for the need that you sense God wants you to lift up in prayer.

These are a few, practical ways that help us to recognize the voice of the Holy Spirit involving Himself in our experiences as we seek to live "naturally supernatural" lives of power and purpose. The list is not meant to be exhaustive, rather it has been designed to help you reflect on ways in which the Spirit of God may be speaking to you.

To paraphrase both CS Lewis and Francis Schaeffer, "God is near and he is not silent!"

Could we stop for a moment and take a quick personal inventory? In which ways that were listed above have you heard the voice of the Holy Spirit? Now that we have learned from the Scripture that Master Jesus speaks to his children by His Holy Spirit in a variety of ways, you now have a framework to process those things the Father wants to share with you today. Since the Spirit speaks through a vast array of means, in what other ways have you heard His voice?

Discovering God's Voice In Your Story

— *Did God speak to you to draw you to Himself when you first became a Christian? If yes, how so?*

— *Has God ever spoken to you through the Bible? If yes, how so?*

— *Has God ever spoken to you through creation? If yes, how so?*

— *Has God ever spoken to you through conversation with another person? If yes, how so?*

— *Has God ever spoken to your heart in a sermon or message given by a minister or teacher? If yes, how so?*

— *Has God ever spoken to your heart through a worship experience? If yes, how so?*

— *Has God ever spoken to you about an issue that you need to make right with Him or others? If yes, how so?*

— *Has God ever spoken to you in affirming you in areas where you truly please Him? If yes, how so?*

— *Has God ever spoken to you by placing on your heart an urge or burden to pray for someone? If yes, how so?*

— *Has God ever spoken to your heart to prompt you to encourage someone? If yes, how so?*

— *Has God ever spoken to you in His still small voice" to give you direction or encouragement? If yes, how so?*

— *Has God ever spoken to you through a dream, a picture, or a vision? If yes, how so?*

If you answered "yes" to any of the questions, how does it make you feel to know that the King of the universe has spoken to you personally? Do you expect God to speak to you? If so, how would you characterize your listening skills? Do you expect God to speak through you to encourage others? Based upon the teaching of the Bible and our own personal experiences, we believe that hearing the voice of the Good Shepherd is the birthright for every child of God. It is intended to be the "normal Christian experience" for every follower of Jesus.

Listening takes practice

As in any other relationship, communication with God must be learned, developed, and practiced. We must "tune our hearts" to God's gracious communication. Though we were never opposed to the idea of letting the Spirit lead our lives by listening to Him, it was also not a facet of our faith that had much emphasis. Most of our prayers involved more talking than listening. Through our connection with the Missional Architects, we slowly came to appreciate and emphasize the leadership of the Holy Spirit. This new reality took time to develop as we practiced hearing together in community. Here are a few of the practices that have been beneficial to us. Explore them. We believe they will benefit you as well.

VERTICAL PRACTICE:
Listening Prayer

Listening to the Holy Spirit with and through His people

We have adapted a prayer exercise created by Tim Keller to help us to pray "conversationally." We can pray this way anytime two or more people gather together. It differs from what is often experienced in group prayer settings in which people either talk in detail about prayer needs leaving little time to actually pray, or offer one prolonged prayer "sermon" after another. We believe that prayer is dialogue and necessarily includes God and others in the process. We invite the Holy Spirit to lead us and expect His encouraging work among us.

The basic guidelines for listening to the Holy Spirit with and through His people:

— Don't take time to share prayer requests unless very briefly. Let them come out as you pray.

— Be brief. Limit yourself to a couple of sentences at a time, covering one thought instead of many.

— Use everyday language.

— Pray spontaneously instead of sequentially going around the circle.

— Build on the prayers of others as in conversation. When a topic is complete, it will be clear by the silence. Anyone can move on to the next topic, not just the leader.

— If a Bible verse comes to mind, do pray it if it seems at all related. This is often how the Holy Spirit confirms our prayers.

— Pray along silently with the one who is praying. Discipline yourself not to be thinking about what you'll pray. Stay actively involved when you are not praying.

— Don't rush to fill a silence. Silences are normal, and can actually be restful.

— If someone is uncomfortable praying aloud, give them the freedom to pray along silently.

— Don't close each prayer "in Jesus' Name, Amen." Assume that every prayer is prayed in His Name. This fosters a continuity or flow in prayer until the very end, when the leader of the group will close in Jesus' Name for the entire prayer session.

— Close the time by asking what people heard from the Lord during the time of prayer.

Time and again, this simple practice of conversational prayer has led to meaningful times of connection with God and one another. We've experienced times of prayer in which the Holy Spirit prompted one person to pray for a need that another group member hadn't shared. There have been times when the Spirit impressed a picture upon one group member during prayer while impressing a confirming Scripture upon another. These times of prayer are faith building for they help us to tangibly experience the leadership of the Holy Spirit.

Listening to the Holy Spirit during individual prayer

While God speaks to us through His community, He also intends to speak to us directly as His individual, treasured children. We see many examples of this throughout the Bible. From Samuel, to David, to Jesus, to Paul we see God speaking to His children individually during times of prayer. Learning to hear the voice of the Holy Spirit requires practice. Here are a number of principles that will help us grow in hearing the voice of the Holy Spirit individually.

— God's voice in our hearts often sounds like our own spontaneous thoughts. While not all of our thoughts are God's communication to us, some of them are indeed.

— Becoming still is helpful so we can sense God's flow of thoughts and emotions within.

— Focusing our hearts upon Jesus by picturing Him, remembering His character and actions, or communing with Him through music.

— Paying attention to words, pictures, and visions that God desires to reveal you.

— Writing down our prayers and God's answers, helps us recognize and become familiar with God's voice.

At one of our gatherings, we were asked to spend time listening to God and afterward share with our families what God said. I didn't hear anything directly from the Lord that day, but my wife did. God spoke with little hoopla or fanfare, just two words that He placed upon Wendy's heart: "patiently and faithfully." God has used those words to anchor us when ministry has been difficult and fruit seemed non-existent. "Patiently and faithfully" encouraged us to take a longview of ministry and not the shortview. How thankful I am for God's gracious words that gave us encouragement and guidance. —Sam

HORIZONTAL PRACTICE:
Speaking God's words to others

In the New Testament, the Bible teaches that God intends His people to encourage others by speaking God's words to them. This practice is called prophecy. 1 Thessalonians 5:19-21 instructs us *"Do not quench the Spirit. Do not despise prophecies, but test everything; hold fast what is good."* These verses give us a few guidelines for correctly speaking God's words to others:

— Humbly speak God's words by saying "I believe that God would have me tell you..." The most common objections to the idea of God speaking through His people today arise in reaction to those who seem to misuse this practice as a means to exert their own agenda or control over someone else. No one should go about claiming they perfectly hear from the Lord. We would be wise to remember that like water traveling through a rusty pipe, we as people can inadvertently taint the perfect words of God with our own hopes, burdens, or perspectives. God is speaking through us, but we sometimes get it wrong. Therefore, we must *humbly* offer to others what God has put on our hearts.

— Test the words spoken by examining the Bible, additional focused prayer, and consulting other mature followers of Jesus.

— Hold on to what is from God. Discard what isn't.

This practice of sharing prophetic insights granted by the Holy Spirit can be incredibly encouraging to the body of Christ in our local congregations as we seek to advance the Kingdom of God and live on mission with Master Jesus. Openness to being used by the Spirit in a prophetic manner can provide opportunities for our personal faith, and the faith of the congregation in which we minister, to grow by leaps and bounds as we witness the supernatural activity of our awesome God manifest in our midst.

> Recently at a prayer gathering my friend Scott and I were tasked with modeling listening prayer for the retreat participants. He shared what was on his heart with me. I then prayed asking God to give me a word of encouragement to bolster my brothers faith. In the silence that followed I felt the Holy Spirit impress upon my heart Joshua chapter one. I felt like I was supposed to share with Scott the phrase, "Be bold and courageous. Don't be afraid for I am with you." I did, and Scott received this word as confirmation of what he believed he had been hearing from the Spirit in his own private devotions. Another pastor from our district came up afterwards and shared that the Holy Spirit had placed that same text on his heart for Scott. Next a woman from Scott's congregation who happened to be at this event came forward and showed us her prayer journal which had an entry of several weeks before where The Holy Spirit had impressed upon her heart that she should pray for her pastor to be "bold and courageous" for the

Lord was going to intercede for him in a significant way. All of these confirmations powerfully affected the retreat participants as they saw God show up in undeniable ways. —*Foye*

Reflection

How often during a week do you take time to listen to God?

When was the last time you sensed God speaking to you specifically? What did He communicate?

What was the last word that God gave you for someone else? What did you do with it?

Chapter 3

STONE THREE
Daily Rhythms
When is the Christian Life Lived?

> For thus said the Lord God, the Holy One of Israel,
> "In returning and rest you shall be saved; in quiet-
> ness and in trust shall be your strength."
> Isaiah 30:15

Growing up in New England, we each spent many summer days swimming in the frigid waters of the Atlantic ocean along the New England coast. We both recall the joy of body surfing in the waves. That experience causes one to feel appropriately small and yet strangely invigorated as you catch a wave and are thrust toward the beach by a force far greater than yourself. As any body surfer knows, the trick to catching an awesome ride is timing the rhythm of the wave. You have to know when to swim hard to match the speed of the incoming swell and when to rest and let the power of the wave shoot you back toward the shore.

Timing is also important when it comes to following Jesus. There are rhythms to life that God has established for us, and at the risk of overusing our metaphor, we have to know when to swim hard and when to rest. If we don't understand the importance of kingdom rhythms and learn to live according to them, we will find ourselves wearing out without getting very far in the journey with Jesus. But when we do learn to live according to God's rhythms, we are swept up in the experience of life-giving rest while also being empowered to accomplish immeasurably more than we could ask or imagine.

THE RHYTHM OF THE DAY

God established rhythms to life beginning with the creation of "the day." After each day of creation it was said that "there was evening and there was morning…" Within every day since creation there has existed this rhythm of "evening and morning." This consistent rhythm shapes the pattern of our lives. Therefore, there is to be a consistent daily rhythm in following Jesus. We see the "dailiness" to the Christian life in Jesus' invitation: *"If anyone would come after me, let him deny himself and take up his cross **daily** and follow me."* (Luke 9:23) The early Christian church lived out this dailiness: *"And **day by day**, attending the temple together and breaking bread in their homes, they received their food with glad and generous hearts, praising God and having favor with all the people. And* *the Lord added to their number **day by day** those who were being saved. (Acts 2:46)*

We also need to follow Jesus daily for our daily rhythms guide our hearts which are forever prone to wander far from our God. This is why the author of Hebrews wisely encouraged the early followers of Jesus to live according to a daily rhythm. *"Take care, brothers, lest there be in any of you an evil, unbelieving heart, leading you to fall away from the living God. But exhort one another **every day**, as long as it is called "today," that none of you may be hardened by the deceitfulness of sin. (Hebrews 3:12-13)* Our hearts are all too easily swayed by distractions and lies and become hardened before we realize it. We can get fooled into thinking that we are living the Christian life when the pattern of our days may reveal that in fact we are not. Tom Johnston, one of our mentors, has said, "Jesus can't be Lord of your life if He isn't Lord of your day."

There is no way around the fact that when we become followers of Jesus, we are called to walk with Him DAILY. This "dailiness" can at times seem less than thrilling. After all, it is the mountain top experience we signed up for, but most of walking with Jesus, like hiking, consists of taking one plodding step after another. Eugene Petersen, pastor and theologian, once wrote that Christianity is designed to be a long walk in the same direction.[16] Don't let this fact discourage you because Jesus walks with us and does some of his very best work in the mundane-ness of our lives. He is as present in the daily rhythms of mealtime prayer, serving our children, diligently laboring in our place of employment, and listening to the hearts of others as He is in an ecstatic worship experience at a church service. As we learn to become aware of Jesus' faithful presence in the daily rhythm, we grow in our ability to faithfully follow Him.

Not only is the day itself a rhythm, but within each day there is a rhythm of rest and activity— "there was evening and there was morning..." Notice how evening is listed first. In the Jewish understanding, the day begins at sundown. The first thing that happens in the day is rest. Therefore, rest is not a reward that we earn by our labor, rather rest is a God given gift from which our labor is intended to flow. That ideas runs completely counter to the performance-oriented thinking of our culture that strives to earn rest in the form of a weekend, vacation, or retirement. That way of life leads to overworking, stress, and sleeplessness because we never seem to be able to accomplish enough to earn the rest we desire. Psalm 127:1-2 describes this futile struggle "Unless the Lord builds the house, those who build it labor in vain. Unless the Lord watches over the city, the watchman stays awake in vain. It is in vain that you rise up early and go late to rest, eating the bread of anxious toil; for he gives to his beloved sleep."

God calls us to reorient our way of life so that our labor flows from resting in Him daily. Jesus invites us, "Come to me, all who labor and are heavy laden, and I will give you rest." (Matthew 11:28) Jesus isn't a greedy boss who is hoping to maximize profits at the laborers' expense. No, He is a loving Savior and Lord who intends to relieve us of the burdens we carry so that we might find rest in Him as He works through us. Jesus told His disciples "Abide in me, and I in you. As the branch cannot bear fruit by itself, unless it abides in the vine, neither can you, unless you *abide in me. I am the vine; you are the branches. Whoever abides in me and I in him, he it is that bears much fruit, for apart from me you can do nothing."* (John 15:4-5) A branch does no work, yet abundant fruit is produced because life flows from the vine out through the branch. In a similar way, as we learn to rest in Christ, we will find that He accomplishes through us what we cannot do on our own. Daily resting in God energizes us for the work He has prepared for us to do within each day.

What does daily resting in Jesus look like? We have already referenced some of the necessary practices in earlier stones: connecting at a heart level with the Lord through the Scriptures, connecting at a heart level with one another, and listening prayer. These practices become particularly powerful in shaping our lives as they become a consistent part of our daily rhythms. Yes, frequency matters. Every single one of us needs "daily bread" both physically and spiritually if we are to thrive.

Friends of ours recently made us aware of a helpful daily practice called CO2 (church of two). The premise is that two people commit to meeting daily and together practicing the two spiritual disciplines of SASHET and Listening Prayer. Each day they meet in person or over the phone and check-in with one another utilizing the SASHET acronym. After sharing the current state of their hearts, they then each share what the Lord is saying to them that day. This assumes that each person is spending time each day in listening prayer. The power of this practice is found in the "dailiness" of transparent fellowship and much needed encouragement.

As we learn to faithfully walk with Jesus, we discover that He transforms our mundane, daily plodding into a *"triumphal procession"* (2 Corinthians 2:14). Jesus is the master of transforming the ordinary into the transcendent. He transforms ordinary earthen water vessels into vats of the choicest wedding wine. He transforms ordinary agricultural activities into soul stirring pictures of God's kingdom. He transforms ordinary bread and wine into the symbols of the New Covenant represented in the communion elements. This is wonderful news because most of life is made up of ordinary, mundane things such as cleaning the house, caring for kids, and driving to work. When we walk with Jesus, mundane activities are no longer merely things we must slog through on our way to the "transcendence" of a weekend, a vacation, a concert, or a church service. These mundane everyday activities become significant opportunities to experience the Living God who speaks. In his classic, *Practicing the Presence of God*, Brother Lawrence wrote about the incredible joy of encountering God through mundane chores such as washing pots as he learned to walk with with Jesus daily. This transformative, daily life in Christ is available to all who will follow Him.

THE RHYTHM OF THE SABBATH

We are called to follow Jesus daily, but not everyday is to be the same. We see this again in the creation account. *"And on the seventh day God finished his work that he had done, and he rested on the seventh day from all his work that he had done. So God blessed the seventh day and made it holy, because on it God rested from all his work that he had done in creation."* (Genesis 2:2-3) The seventh day of the week was different than the previous six. It was made "holy", meaning set apart from the other days by God's rest.

When God rested on the Sabbath, it was not because He was exhausted and needed a break. God never tires and never ceases His redemptive work. Jesus made it clear that God works on the Sabbath. When Jesus was questioned as to why He was working one Sabbath day He stated, *"My Father is working until now, and I am working."* (John 5:17) God's rest on the seventh day of creation is meant to demonstrate something about His Kingdom. In ancient cultures, a king's throne was referred to as his "seat of rest." Consider Acts 7:49, *"Heaven is my throne, and the earth is my footstool. What kind of house will you build for me, says the Lord, or what is the place of my rest?"* When God rested on the seventh day, he was declaring that He is not only Creator, but is also the all powerful King seated on His throne, ruling over all that He has made. God established the rhythm of Sabbath rest as a tangible way for His people to remember He is both Creator and King.

This weekly pattern of labor and rest became one of the primary marks distinguishing God's chosen people from all the nations which surrounded them. The Israelites were to follow God's command to "remember the Sabbath day to keep it holy." While the Gentile nations labored seven days a week to provide for themselves, the Israelites declared their trust in God to provide for them by resting on the Sabbath as God had commanded.

This weekly pattern was established by God not to be a pointless test but to be a beneficial rhythm needed by humanity in order to truly flourish. However, humanity has rarely viewed it as such. For instance, during the French Revolution the government attempted to replace the seven day week with a ten day week. It was an attempt to increase productivity while removing the religious foundations upon which the society was built. The ten day week was a disaster. People weren't designed to live according to that exhausting rhythm.

All too often, our view of the Sabbath is similar to the perspective of the French government. It can seem like a nuisance, a hinderance, or a divinely imposed "nap time." When viewed this way, few want to keep the Sabbath. But God's intentions for the Sabbath are not what we fear. He intends for us to enjoy a weekly "holyday" that renews the body and realigns the soul to the values of God's Kingdom. The Sabbath is not intended to be an end unto itself. It's purpose is to keep our lives in alignment with the values of God's kingdom so that our daily lives are characterized by worship, generosity, and celebration.

The Sabbath: A Rhythm of Worship

The Sabbath is an opportunity to experience rest and realign our lives through worshipping God. Worship is about recognizing and glorifying someone or something's worth. Whether we are religious or not, we all worship. Everyone judges the worth of people, possessions, sports teams, hobbies, scenery, etc. and then glorifies what they deem worthy. We have different opinions of what is worthy, but we all worship. It is isn't wrong to recognize and glorify the worth of things other than God. God made all things for us to enjoy. For instance, we should recognize the worth of our spouse and rightly worship. Historic wedding vows contained this sentiment: "with my body, I thee worship." However, it is both wrong and foolish to glorify anything or anyone else as our God. Only God is worthy of our ultimate worship for only He can meet our ultimate needs.

The great problem of humanity lies in the fact that we all undervalue God's worth and overvalue the worth of the things God has made. As a result we *worship and serve created things rather than the Creator."* (Romans 1:25) We overvalue created things such as romantic love, a career, physical appearance, family, others' approval, or financial success by looking to those things for our significance, security, and joy. When we do this, these created things become "functional gods." They usurp God's place in our life. When someone or something becomes a "functional god" in our life, that person or thing ceases to be a gift that we enjoy but becomes a "source" from which we are trying to draw life. This reality is even expressed in popular phrasing when people say things like: "his job is his life", "basketball is her life", or "her kids are her life." These statements may accurately reflect how we are living, but they also reveal how incredibly foolish we can become when we allow God's good gifts to displace His person in our affections. Nothing apart from God can impart life. Instead, other things force us to give our life to them but they can impart no real life in return. The end result of glorifying other people or things as our "functional god" is not rest, but worry, stress, and disappointment.

Therefore, we need a rhythm of worship that realigns our life to God's worth so that we won't live under the tyranny of the other "gods" that we are tempted to foolishly glorify. We need to be regularly reminded of God's greatness, drink in His goodness, gaze upon His beauty, and thereby recognize His unsurpassing worth. This is why when the Israelites left their slavery in Egypt, God gave them instructions for a new way of life that revolved around a calendar built upon a rhythm of worship. The weekly Sabbath, feasts and holy days were meant to reorient God's people towards His worth so that they would gratefully live under His gracious rule. It was not only the Old Testament people of God who lived according to a rhythm of worship, but the New Testament believers also. Very early on in the life of the church, followers of Jesus began gathering on the first day of each week to celebrate the resurrection victory of King Jesus that happened on a Sunday. The day of the week that we worship on, is not as important as the fact that we gather weekly to worship.

Our souls need a regular rhythm of worship that we might be reminded of what is true and be inspired by the God who is true. This gathering may happen in a cathedral, a home, a traditional church building, a storefront, a pub, or coffee shop. The point is not the setting of our worship, but in exalting the One who is said to "inhabit the praises of His people." As we engage in a regular Sabbath rhythm of worship, our souls are renewed and realigned so that we might live our daily lives glorifying God.

The Sabbath: A Rhythm of Generosity

One of the greatest barriers to experiencing God's rest is our relationship to money. We overvalue money and therefore overwork in order to accumulate more of it. In the thick fog of our seemingly unending exhaustion, we can even find ourselves dreaming about or creating schemes to gain it apart from legitimate work. We deeply fear not having enough money and therefore spend many of our non-working hours worrying about financial matters. We desire for ourselves the amount of money others possess and become discontent with the amount of money that God has entrusted to us to steward well for Him. We get into crazy disputes over money, which then causes great friction within our relationships, particularly among family members. If we are to experience the rest God longs to give us, then we desperately need something to change with regard to our relationship to money. As has been often said, "money can be a wonderful servant, but its a terrible master."

God desires that we rest in His provision rather than "*eating the bread of anxious toil*" (Psalm 127:2). Our hearts must be formed to receive the daily bread that our Father gives us rather than craving that which He does not offer. In order to form the hearts of His people, God calls us to practice grace filled, Spirit-led giving, and avoid the temptation to embrace the lifestyle of constant accumulation. The ancient Israelites practiced this type of giving in a number of ways. They brought offerings to the Temple in the form of animal sacrifices, food offerings, and monetary offerings. They also made it a regular habit to practice generosity by giving to the poor.

Jesus affirmed how necessary generosity is in forming our hearts if we are to experience God's Kingdom rule. Jesus urges His followers not to be consumed with worry over financial matters, but rather to *"seek first the kingdom of God and his righteousness, and all these things will be added to you."* (Matthew 6:33) The word "righteousness" means "right relationship." It refers to the practice of giving to the poor. Jesus is teaching His disciples that the way to cease worrying over financial matters is to practice generosity, trusting in our Great King to meet our every need. Jesus taught that the practice of giving is not intended to be a divine tax to fill up God's bank account, but rather is a divine grace that results in true rest for God's beloved people.

While generosity should be practiced at various times at the spontaneous prompting of the Holy Spirit, there is also great wisdom in adopting a basic rhythm of generosity that helps bring Kingdom of God principles to bear on how we manage our finances. Developing a basic rhythm of giving forms our hearts to be even more receptive to the Holy Spirit as he prompts us to meet the needs of those whom God loves.

God commanded those who followed him in the Old Testament to observe a specific rhythm of generosity by calling them to give him the "firstfruits" of their harvest. What a trust forming rhythm! Though they weren't sure if a storm would come and ruin the rest of the crop, they gave him their best at the very beginning of the harvest season, thereby demonstrating their trust that their Creator King would provide for them and for those they loved. The Apostle Paul also encouraged a regular rhythm of New Testament generosity when he directed the followers of Jesus in Corinth: *"On the first day of every week, each one of you should set aside a sum of money in keeping with your income..."* (1 Corinthians 16:2 NLT). This giving was not to be a grating duty, but rather an act of joyful worship. He goes on to share with these very same disciples that *"Each one must give as he has decided in his heart, not reluctantly or under compulsion, for God loves a cheerful giver"* (2 Corinthians 9:7). This rhythm of joyful giving formed the routines of worship and generosity in the very first disciples. This rhythm of generosity has continued to shape each generation of disciples who have followed in the Corinthian disciples' faith filled footsteps. Jesus' followers of today are also graciously offered the liberating joy that comes from rejecting the practice of calculating down to the penny how much of our Savior's money we can keep, and instead embrace a lifestyle which actively seeks to give more and more of Christ's incredible largesse away so that His Kingdom will be advanced.

If we believe that everything we have belongs to the Lord Jesus and has been freely given to us according to His abundant mercy and grace, what changes do we need to make to develop a rhythm of grace filled, Spirit led generosity? First, we must remember that we who have experienced God's forgiveness are no longer bound to the Old Testament law. We have been set free from having to give out of compulsion. We can now experience the incredible joy that erupts out of giving to God from the wellspring of our great love for Him. This sacrificial love for God then overflows out from us as we love others and meet their needs out of our super-abundance. Secondly, Jesus never commanded His disciples to tithe. We are commanded to move from the Old Testament percentage to a New Testament proportion. As we make more, we get to give more away! This freedom we receive in the Gospel from the tyranny of money keeps us from adopting "lifestyle inflation;" whereby we spend more on ourselves as we make more money. Kingdom servants are given Kingdom resources for Kingdom purposes! Thirdly, we embrace Kingdom generosity as we meet the needs of the poor. Unlike the Old Testament faithful, we don't cap our contribution towards meeting the needs of the poor at a certain prescribed percentage. Instead we look to meet what ever needs we can as the needs arise. This is Gospel driven generosity. Lastly, we are invited to invest in causes which will pay dividends in eternity, not only in the here and now. Listen to Paul words as he exhorts the church at Ephesus.

> For the one who sows to his own flesh will from the flesh reap corruption, but the one who sows to the Spirit will from the Spirit reap eternal life. And let us not grow weary of doing good, for in due season we will reap, if we do not give up. So then, as we have opportunity, let us do good to everyone, and especially to those who are of the household of faith. Ephesians 6:8-10

When was the last time we asked ourselves in a moment of complete transparency and truth, "What opportunities do I have to support the in-breaking of the Kingdom right here and right now?" It is in asking that question of God's

Spirit that He speaks to our hearts and provides direction so that our precious funds are spent well and wisely.

Our friend Gary Hoag summarizes the Kingdom perspective on money well when he says;

> I am finding that God's love is what empowers me to empty myself in service to others; that participating with God in his work by sharing generously with my spiritual leaders brings me joy; that remembering the poor, especially Christian brothers and sisters, is one of the most meaningful privileges of my life; and, the only way to take hold of eternal life is to let go of all that is in this earthly one.[17]

Today's disciples need a regular rhythm of generosity to form our hearts in relationship to money. We shouldn't think that we must give money every time we gather to worship God. There is freedom for each of us to discern exactly what our regular rhythm will be. But whatever the rhythm you decide to adopt, it will provide a needed pathway of heart formation that will lead to rest. As we practice a regular rhythm of giving, we will find our lives increasingly marked by deeper contentment and greater generosity instead of debilitating worry and consuming greed.

As author Randy Alcorn once famously said, "God is far more interested in raising your standard of giving than your standard of living."

The Sabbath: A Rhythm of Celebration

Celebration is a vital component in experiencing the rest God intends and has always played an important role in God's way of life. Through weekly Sabbath and yearly festivals, the Israelites celebrated the saving activities of God. These days were set apart as holy from the other days to both remember and anticipate. If we are to walk with Jesus, then we also must learn the importance of celebrating "holydays" that we will both remember what God has done and anticipate what God will do.

Celebration helps us to remember the incredible demonstrations of His power and love that God has orchestrated on our behalf. The failures of the Israelites to follow God's way of life were quite often grounded in a failure to remember what He had done in the past. When they forgot how he had delivered and provided for them, they were inclined to doubt His power and goodness in the present. For that reason, God commanded them to establish a rhythm of feasts and festivals that celebrated His saving activities. Every year, the Israelites would celebrate the Passover remembering how the judgment of God had passed over them in Egypt and how His grace had delivered their firstborn children from certain death. Every year they would celebrate the Festival of Booths during which they would camp out remembering that their ancestors had wandered in the wilderness until God had brought them to their home in the Promised Land. Every year they would celebrate the Feast of Weeks remembering that God had given them His Covenant Law on Mt Sinai.

The Sabbath was also listed in Leviticus 23 as one of the festivals to be celebrated once the Israelites entered the Promised Land. Celebratory feasts have always been, and always will be central to God's plan for His people to remember His saving activities.

Celebration also helps us to anticipate what God will do. While we do experience Kingdom life now under Jesus' rule, the Bible tells us it is only a "foretaste." What we will ultimately experience is a wedding feast, victory party, family reunion, and coronation all rolled into one massive celebration. Thankfully, our eternal rest has nothing to do with playing a harp on a wispy cloud, but rather entails a joint ruling over all creation with Jesus in the midst of joyful celebration. This is the rest that we need and for which we ultimately long.

Though we both are from New England, we are divided in our respective baseball team loyalties. Foye roots for the Yankees. Sam is an avid Red Sox fan. Much to Sam's delight (and Foye's chagrin), not only did the Yankees not make the playoffs in 2013, but the Red Sox went on to win the World Series. During the ninth inning of game six in the World Series, it became quite apparent that the Red Sox were going to win the Series. Boston fans were on their feet wildly cheering, anticipating victory. Red Sox superstar David Ortiz had donned His celebratory goggles and helmet in Boston's dugout. Though the game was not yet over, the party had already begun.

In a similar manner, the heavenly celebration has already begun for those whose King is Jesus Christ. No, the game is not over yet. Though we still experience sin, sorrow, and suffering; we can't help but rejoice and celebrate for the eternal party has already begun.

By establishing regular rhythms of Sabbath celebration and holiday festivals, followers of Jesus can joyfully anchor their lives in what Jesus has already done and confidently anticipate what He will do. Celebration is crucial for it helps form our lives to the rhythms of God's Kingdom rather than the rhythms of this world. As we adopt the rhythms of heaven, we begin to find the rest that our souls crave. As a friend of ours named Jason has said, "Restlessness is the atmosphere of hell, rest is the atmosphere of heaven."

How can we rest when we are so restless?

If we are to faithfully follow Jesus for the long haul, then we need to live according to the rhythms of the day and the sabbath. In observing these rhythms, we can experience the rejuvenating rest that God offers to any who will receive it. However, we all struggle mightily to conform our lives to God's rhythms. There is so much going on seemingly all the time that life just has a way of filling all our available time. Despite good intention and great effort, we struggle to consistently maintain Kingdom rhythms in our lives.

So what then are we to do? Try harder? Try new technology to manage our time better? Though there is something to be said for arranging our calendars around what we say is most important, that's not where we're headed. The core issue that keeps us from resting in God's rhythms isn't primarily a time management issue, it's a heart issue. Deep down in our souls we are restless making it all but impossible to establish consistent rhythms of rest.

In Isaiah 30:15, we read God's description of His people's restlessness, "*For thus said the Lord God, the Holy One of Israel, 'In returning and rest you shall be saved; in quietness and in trust shall be your strength.' But you were unwilling.*" God has been calling humanity to rest in Him, but we have been unwilling to receive the rest He offers. The plot-line of the Bible and the experience of our lives shows us that we are a restless people who are unwilling to rest in our Creator King. Like toddlers who are thoroughly exhausted but refuse to take a nap, we need someone to settle and soothe our restlessness.

Jesus is our Sabbath Rest

Since we are unwilling to go to God for rest, Jesus has brought this rest to us. When we receive Him as our Savior, we are enabled by the Holy Spirit to truly rest. Let's explore how Jesus accomplished this.

In the Jewish week, Friday is the day of preparation for the Sabbath. On that day, people would labor in their homes, beating lumps of dough to prepare their bread so that on the Sabbath, they could rest. One particular Friday, Jesus labored up a hill, after others had beaten his body to prepare Him for crucifixion. The next day, on the Sabbath, He would also rest— in death. Death is referred to as rest in the Bible, but never in a good way. Proverbs 21:16 says *"One who wanders from the way of good sense will **rest** in the assembly of the dead."* Jesus hadn't foolishly wandered away from God's path. We have. We don't have the sense to trust God and rest in Him. We foolishly slave away eating the bread of anxious toil, thinking our efforts can bring us rest. They cannot. The only work that can truly bring rest to our souls was done by Jesus as He hung on the cross. When He uttered the words— "It is finished," He completed the only work that can bring an end to our restless wanderings.

Then on the Sabbath, while God's people kept the letter of the Sabbath law, resting in their homes and synagogues, Jesus fulfilled it while resting in His tomb. Lying there doing nothing, he accomplished everything. His rest is our salvation.

As in Creation, there was evening and then there was morning. The Creator King emerged from His rest with the assembly of the dead as Lord over death so that we may become the assembly of those who rest in His life. Jesus now invites us to enter the rest for which we were made. Listen to the teaching of Hebrews 4:9-10 *"So then, there remains a Sabbath rest for the people of God, for whoever has entered God's rest has also rested from his works as God did from his."* St Augustine of Hippo spoke of this very same rest when He prayed, "Thou hast made us for thyself, O Lord, and our hearts are restless until they find their rest in Thee."

When we place our faith in Jesus and His finished work, we cease our anxious strivings and attempts to impress others. We stop trying to impress God and others by what we can do since God is already pleased with us because of the work Jesus has done. We stop trying to ensure our own security by earning enough money to protect ourselves against disaster since we have all that we need for life and godliness in Christ. We stop needing to fill our time with endless activity in a vain attempt to feel significant for Jesus has given us true significance enabling us to rest.

From this place of rest in Christ, we are freed to live out our daily rhythms. We do not need to earn anything, because in Christ, we have already received everything we need. We can receive His presence, power, and peace daily. We can receive the blessings of fellowship, hope, and renewal each week. God's rhythms bring true rest to our weary souls.

VERTICAL PRACTICE:
Morning Prayer of Devotion

Many Christians throughout history have found the practice of morning prayer to be essential for walking with Jesus and becoming like Him. We see the practice of morning prayer in the Psalms. *"Satisfy us in the morning with your steadfast love, that we may rejoice and be glad all our days."* (Psalm 90:14) *"It is good to give thanks to the Lord, to sing praises to your name, O Most High; to declare your steadfast love in the morning, and your faithfulness by night."* (Psalm 92:1-2) We see Jesus engaging in this practice regularly: *"And rising very early in the morning, while it was still dark, he departed and went out to a desolate place, and there he prayed."* (Mark 1:35)

For the Psalmist and for Jesus, it was essential to receive fresh expression of God's love and to yield themselves to God's rule each morning.

You may ask "Why morning?" We think CS Lewis answers the question well:

> *It comes the very moment you wake up each morning. All your wishes and hopes for the day rush at you like wild animals. And the first job each morning consists simply in shoving them all back; in listening to that other voice, taking that other point of view, letting that other larger, stronger, quieter life come flowing in. And so on, all day. Standing back from all your natural fussings and frettings; coming in out of the wind.*[18]

Most days do not begin with the wonderful awareness of how much God loves us, how lovely God is, or how His image is reflected in others. Other worries and temptations crowd these great truths out. Therefore, we must devote ourselves each day to the reality of the Kingdom of God. As we develop a rhythm of devotion to Jesus each morning, we will find that we agree with the Psalmist when he asserts that it is good to declare God's steadfast love in the morning and His faithfulness each night.

If you are looking for a pattern on which to base this time of prayer, we suggest praying through the affirmations listed in Chapter Two under "Vertical Practices" which describe the essential aspects of living in God's Kingdom.

HORIZONTAL PRACTICE:
Rhythms of Rest

The practice of Sabbath has a vertical dimension in that we recognize God's rule by resting. Yet, Jesus made it clear that Sabbath is for our benefit not God's (Mark 2:27). The Sabbath is intended to have a horizontal impact in our lives and the world around us. The Sabbath encourages generosity for on that day we make a choice to rest from laboring for own income, and instead give offerings when we gather to worship. The Sabbath produces fertile opportunity for relationship by creating a "holyday" on which to gather and celebrate. The Sabbath also creates a powerful opportunity for witness in that we declare with our rest that "Jesus is King, and we trust in Him."

As you prayerfully consider how and when you will practice the Sabbath, we suggest these aspects should be part of your Sabbath practice:

1. Gathering with other followers of Jesus to worship.
2. Financial Generosity through sacrificial giving.
3. Celebration by doing something special, enjoyable, and life-giving that makes the Sabbath a "holyday."

Reflection

Describe your practice of the Sabbath, putting a rhythm of rest and worship into your life?

Describe your practice of giving, putting a rhythm of generosity into your life.

What role does celebration play in your life? How is it intentional?

Chapter 4

STONE FOUR

Family as Church, Church as Family

With Whom Are We to Follow Jesus?

All praise to God, the Father of our Lord Jesus Christ, who has blessed us with every spiritual blessing in the heavenly realms because we are united with Christ. Even before he made the world, God loved us and chose us in Christ to be holy and without fault in his eyes. God decided in advance to adopt us into his own family by bringing us to himself through Jesus Christ. This is what he wanted to do, and it gave him great pleasure. So we praise God for the glorious grace he has poured out on us who belong to his dear Son.
Ephesians 1:3-5 NLT

Ask people what their happiest experiences in life have been, and you'll usually hear a family story of some sort. Maybe it was the memory of a wedding day, a birth, a holiday celebration, or a family vacation. Ask people what their saddest experiences have been and you'll likely hear another family story of some kind. Possibly it is the memory of a loved one's death, or parents divorcing, or loneliness, or abuse, or abandonment. For good or for ill, our lives are profoundly shaped by family. This reveals something fundamental about life. We are wired to belong to a family.

God's story is not only about the glory of His Kingdom, but also about the passionate love He has for His royal family. God has always existed in family relationship within Himself: Father, Son, and Holy Spirit. God didn't create humanity because He was lonely and needed company. He created humanity to be part of His family. The King of the universe created us to be His dearly loved children.

But as you no doubt know by your own life experience, our relationship with God hasn't been all hugs and happiness. This family story has involved heart wrenching dysfunction and intentional separation. Jesus once described the goodness of God's heart by telling a story of family brokenness that we have come to call the story of The Prodigal Son.

> *There was once a man who had two sons. The younger said to his father, "Father, I want right now what's coming to me." So the father divided the property between them. It wasn't long before the younger son packed his bags and left for*

a distant country. There, undisciplined and dissipated, he wasted everything he had. After he had gone through all his money, there was a bad famine all through that country and he began to hurt. He signed on with a citizen there who assigned him to his fields to slop the pigs. He was so hungry he would have eaten the corncobs in the pig slop, but no one would give him any.

That brought him to his senses. He said, "All those farmhands working for my father sit down to three meals a day, and here I am starving to death. I'm going back to my father. I'll say to him, Father, I've sinned against God, I've sinned before you; I don't deserve to be called your son. Take me on as a hired hand." He got right up and went home to his father.

When he was still a long way off, his father saw him. His heart pounding, he ran out, embraced him, and kissed him. The son started his speech: "Father, I've sinned against God, I've sinned before you; I don't deserve to be called your son ever again."

But the father wasn't listening. He was calling to the servants, "Quick. Bring a clean set of clothes and dress him. Put the family ring on his finger and sandals on his feet. Then get a grain-fed heifer and roast it. We're going to feast! We're going to have a wonderful time! My son is here—given up for dead and now alive! Given up for lost and now found!" And they began to have a wonderful time.

All this time his older son was out in the field. When the day's work was done he came in. As he approached the house, he heard the music and dancing. Calling over one of the houseboys, he asked what was going on. He told him, "Your brother came home. Your father has ordered a feast— barbecued beef!—because he has him home safe and sound."

The older brother stalked off in an angry sulk and refused to join in. His father came out and tried to talk to him, but he wouldn't listen. The son said, "Look how many years I've stayed here serving you, never giving you one moment of grief, but have you ever thrown a party for me and my friends? Then this son of yours who has thrown away your money on whores shows up and you go all out with a feast!"

His father said, "Son, you don't understand. You're with me all the time, and everything that is mine is yours—but this is a wonderful time, and we had to celebrate. This brother of yours was dead, and he's alive! He was lost, and he's found!"
Luke 15:11-32 *The Message*

As Tim Keller points out in his book *The Prodigal God*,[19] both boys resented their father. Both boys are looking for their father's wealth, not looking to share in their father's love. Both boys insulted their father and removed themselves from His presence. As hard as it is, we must recognize that this is our story as well. We have all caused brokenness in our relationship with God. Some of us have been more like the younger brother: rejecting God by obviously breaking His rules. Others have been more like the older brother: more subtly rejecting God's heart by thinking that our moral performance earns us an inheritance. It really doesn't matter which sin we choose, both result in a broken family dynamic.

But the focus of Jesus' story is not on the sin of the boys, but the love of the Father. The Father's heart is unbelievably good. He doesn't treat the boys as they deserved. He bears the cost of their rebellion both financially and emotionally. He returns acceptance for their rejection and love for their disdain. Instead of calling His sons to account, he calls them to a family table of grace. This fictional family represents the family of mercy, grace, and love for which we were made, the Holy Trinity itself.

By grace, the Father's love has been lavished upon us and we are now called children of God— and that is what we are! We need to regularly remind ourselves of this family reality that we described in Stone One. When we put our faith in Jesus, His Father becomes ours. This Heavenly Father is a dad whose love for us is steadfast. He is a Father who delights to give good gifts to His children. He is a Father whose discipline is always just and beneficial. God has committed Himself to us to be our Father and desires that we relate to Him in this familiar way.

Now, if we have become sons and daughters of the Father, that means we also have new brothers and sisters who will remain our siblings forever. Each and every one of us who has trusted in Christ as our Savior has been adopted by a Dad who loves His family, and who desires that His family love both Him and one another sacrificially.

When we understand that the Christian story is a family story, we will come to see that it is impossible to view our relationship with Jesus merely in individual terms alone.

Now, this is a challenge for western Christians to believe and live because of our highly individualized culture that views faith as a personal matter. Within western Christian culture, we frequently view our relationship with God as a "personal relationship" just between an individual and God. This view has led many people to attempt to live in relationship with God while having little to no relationship with their eternal brothers and sisters.

> I remember taking my two daughters to the Daddy Daughter Valentines Dance at their elementary school. We got all dressed up. Pinned on flowers. Took our pictures. We looked like a wonderfully happy family. But when we arrived at the school and began to dance together, the happy faces seen in the pictures began to change. My daughters' dancing styles are very different. One wanted to spend the evening doing graceful spins, the other wanted jump around and wrestle. These styles weren't very compatible and therefore my daughters began to each vie for the opportunity to dance without the other. While I deeply love and appreciate both of my daughters and their unique styles, it broke my heart to see their differences causing division in our family. The result of their division was that in separating from each other, they not only pulled away from one another, but they pulled away from me. —*Sam*

The apostle John described the relational dynamic that exists within our Heavenly Father's family in a similar way:

If anyone says, "I love God," and hates his brother, he is a liar; for he who does not love his brother whom he has seen cannot love God whom he has not seen. And this commandment we have from him: whoever loves God must also love his brother.
1 John 4:19-21

John is saying that we can't be in fellowship with the Father, but be out of fellowship with His family. It just doesn't work that way. Loving God involves loving His other kids also.

Here's what this boils down to: we cannot follow Jesus alone because following Jesus isn't a solo hike, it is a family trip. Life in God's Kingdom is lived with God's family. If we find ourselves journeying all alone, then we must conclude that we have left the trail. The way of Jesus must be walked with family.

It's one thing to talk about following Jesus as a family, it's quite another thing to live it. When you combine our fast past culture, impersonal church structures, and relational disappointments we experience at the hands of other Christians, it seems like a pipe-dream to think of being able to follow Jesus together in any real family sense. So, what then are we to do?

Our families are to be "little churches."

What if following Jesus with others wasn't primarily about adding more relationships and activities into your already over crowded life. What if the "others" that Jesus wants you to walk with are the people you already do life with?

That's an incredibly freeing thought, isn't it? This perspective we are championing isn't a trendy, anti-institutional model of church picked up at a conference somewhere. This has been God's heart for how His community was to function since the very beginning.

Consider Moses' words found in Deuteronomy 6:1-9:

> *"Now this is the commandment—the statutes and the rules—that the Lord your God commanded me to teach you, that you may do them in the land to which you are going over, to possess it, that you may fear the Lord your God, you and your son and your son's son, by keeping all his statutes and his commandments, which I command you, all the days of your life, and that your days may be long. Hear therefore, O Israel, and be careful to do them, that it may go well with you, and that you may multiply greatly, as the Lord, the God of your fathers, has promised you, in a land flowing with milk and honey.*
>
> *"Hear, O Israel: The Lord our God, the Lord is one. You shall love the Lord your God with all your heart and with all your soul and with all your might. And these words that I command you today shall be on your heart. You shall teach them diligently to your children, and shall talk of them when you sit in your house, and when you walk by the way, and when you lie down, and when you rise. You shall bind them as a sign on your hand, and they shall be as frontlets between your eyes. You shall write them on the doorposts of your house and on your gates."*

In this passage, Moses is passing on instruction from God as to how the Israelites are to follow Him and pass on God's way of life from generation to generation once they cross over into the promised land. The parents, not the priests, are given the task of teaching the next generation who God is and how they were to follow His ways. The home, not the Tabernacle, is the setting for this instruction. Though corporate worship was an essential part of God's way of life, God didn't instruct parents to get their kids to church to learn His way of life. Rather He instructed parents to, in essence, be the church at home!!

We also see the family functioning as a "little church" in the New Testament. Consider Ephesians 6:1-4:

> Children, obey your parents in the Lord, for this is right. "Honor your father and mother" (this is the first commandment with a promise), "that it may go well with you and that you may live long in the land." Fathers, do not provoke your children to anger, but bring them up in the discipline and instruction of the Lord.

It was primarily the parents, not a sunday school teacher or youth pastor, that taught children the way of Jesus. The family unit functioned as a "little church."

During the middle 1700's the First Great Awakening swept across New England. Pastor, philosopher, and theologian Jonathan Edwards was a key leader in this movement. Many people remember him for his famous sermons and writings. Though Edwards championed the value of the gathered church, he viewed the role of the family to be of the greatest importance:

> *Every Christian family ought to be as it were a little church, consecrated to Christ, and wholly influenced and governed by his rules. And family education and order are some of the chief means of grace. If these fail, all other means are likely to prove ineffectual. If these are duly maintained, all the means of grace will be likely to prosper and be successful.*[20]

Consider the power of Christians viewing their families as little churches and their homes as places of worship, discipleship and mission. Worshipping God would not be limited to a Sunday morning experience in a church building, but would be part of the natural flow of family life— around the dinner table, in the car, while doing chores. Discipleship would not be confined to curriculum taught in a classroom at a church building, but would be done as God brings along daily teaching opportunities in the curriculum of life. Mission would not be reduced to a task done by missionaries in a foreign country, but would be the life of Jesus shining through a family to their friends, family, co-workers, classmates, and neighbors. Just imagine the power of dozens or even hundreds of family "churches" in a town, each being a community of worship, discipleship, and mission. The family functioning as the church has the power for the life of Christ to go *deep* into the lives of those within each family as they live all of life as the church instead of only going to church one hour a week. The family functioning as the church also has the power for the life of Christ to go *wide* into the lives of other families in our communities as many people unexpectedly encounter Jesus as these "family churches" go about their natural lives.

While the vision of families functioning as little churches may sound appealing, it may also raise a number of questions and fears. What if you are single? What if you live with a group of friends not a biological family? What if you are the only follower of Jesus in your family? What if you want your family to function in this way, but your kids are almost grown and you don't see how it can be accomplished with the time left to you?

Our churches are to be "larger families."

Thankfully, God has provided a larger "family" to which we all belong forever to encourage and instruct us. So even if your household family can't function as a little church at this moment, we still have a larger family with whom we can follow Jesus. All followers of Jesus make up God's larger family which in Scripture is called the "church." In Scripture, the "church" is never referred to as a building, organization, or worship service. The church is always used in reference to people— the people who make up God's family.

Unfortunately many people today have had experiences of being in churches that seemed to be anything but a healthy family. Some churches function more like a dysfunctional family who are always fighting, while others function like an impersonal business where there aren't any real relationships. There are plenty of negative examples of churches failing to function as the family of God. When you combine these negative church experiences with the rampant individualism and consumerism of our culture, you have a witch's brew of dissatisfaction and disappointment with the institutional church which is being drunk deeply in our day. People are leaving the established church in droves in favor of enjoying a more "personal" faith; a personal faith that is free from the inconvenience of dealing with other people's shortcomings and idiosyncrasies.

In looking at the dysfunction of the organized church, some may think this departure to be a good thing. We would would say it is not. Dissociating from the body of Christ because of the problems within the church is similar to amputating an arm in an attempt to keep it from becoming infected by a disease residing elsewhere within the body. The cure then becomes worse than the problem. Cut off from the body of Christ, we end up being cut off from the life of Christ for which we long.

Dissociation from God's family is not only a temptation for modern, western Christians. This temptation to remove one's self from the difficulties found within body life has been present in every age. That is why Hebrews 10:24-25 counsels Christ's followers to … *consider how to stir up one another to love and good works, not neglecting to meet together, as is the habit of some, but encouraging one another, and all the more as you see the Day drawing near.*

Healthy families gather together regularly. In fact they eagerly look forward to doing so. They gather to celebrate, grieve, encourage, and recreate. In calling us to not neglect gathering together, God isn't telling us to make sure we get our weekly dose of preaching. He is telling us to value getting together with our eternal brothers and sisters. We're family, we need to get together often!

While we do benefit from these family gatherings, our personal benefit is not the primary reason we are called to gather. The author of Hebrews didn't say, "if you neglect meeting together you won't be spiritually encouraged." Instead, he wrote that our reason to gather was to encourage one another. Healthy families gather for the benefit of the others. They gather to bring comfort to the grieving. They gather to add to the joy of the couple getting married. They gather to provide encouragement to the discouraged. We are called by our Father to stir up and encourage our brothers and sisters to demonstrate love and undertake good works. This is the way of Jesus. He did not come to be served, but to serve others. When we realize how Jesus has served us, drawing us into His family at the cost of His own life, we begin to serve others in response to Jesus. This is how God's family works.

When we as God's family gather to encourage one another, we connect to our larger forever family who encourages, inspires and instructs us as to how our household families can better function as little churches.

Now, in holding high the value of being connected with the church, we are not wishing for a return to the "good ole days" of Christendom when it was assumed that most people would "go to church." Nor are we issuing a call to "do church better" so that our services and programs will woo all the people back who have turned their backs on the church. We are calling people to experience Jesus in His family. No matter a church's model, style, or structure; if the Spirit of Jesus is within the people of that church, then the church has the potential to function as God's family.

If we are to follow Jesus with our household families and church families, then we need practices that make this family reality tangible.

VERTICAL PRACTICE:
Family worship

Early on in the development of the Five Stones, God impressed upon us the necessity of living out this way of life first and foremost with our household families. Since both of us are pastors, we know all too well the danger of seeking to lead others in Christ while neglecting the spiritual life of our own families. This all too common approach is backwards to the teaching of the New Testament which makes proper nurture of the spiritual life in the household family one of the primary qualifications for leadership within the larger church family. As Tom Johnston and Mike Perkinson are fond of saying, "If it doesn't work at home, we don't get to export it."

So over the past few years, we have been very intentional to set aside time to worship God with our families. During this time of worship, we are simply trying to live out with our families some of the core practices we have already described. We connect at a heart level with the Lord through the Scriptures and we pray together— pouring out our hearts to God and listening for His words to us.

The practice of family worship is highly flexible and easily contoured to the schedule, season of life, and personality of a family. Some families set aside a time every day in the morning to meet with God. Others set aside an evening once a week. Some families with younger children utilize a children's resource like *The Jesus Storybook Bible* by Sally Lloyd Jones.[21] Others spend individual time in the Scriptures and gather to share what God is revealing to them. Some families sing hymns or listen to worship music. Others recite creeds, answer catechetical questions or pray historic prayers together. The frequency and content of family worship must be determined by each family as the Spirit directs.

Family worship also is to be practiced with our larger church family. By "family worship" we don't mean simply "going to church" as it has frequently been practiced in our culture. Too often, attending a worship service is little more than individual spectators gathering to hear one person speak rather than a family who gathers to worship God and encourage their siblings each with their own unique contribution. That is the picture of a worship service that we see describe in 1 Corinthians 14:26 *"What then, brothers? When you come together, each one has a hymn, a lesson, a revelation, a tongue, or an interpretation. Let all things be done for building up."* In a gathered family of worshippers, there is real participation (with a diversity of gifting) from all present. This results in the building up of God's church, which is His family.

HORIZONTAL PRACTICE:
Family Table

In our day, eating is little more than fueling up to keep our bodies on the run. We shove food into our mouths while we are on the go so that we can be as productive as possible. Eating was different for Jesus. Eating wasn't just a time for fueling up, but for fellowship. Table fellowship played a central role in Jesus' life and ministry. He was constantly connecting with people over a meal. At the table, Jesus revealed the depth of God's love through the communion celebration with His disciples and the breadth of God's love at table fellowship with tax collectors and Pharisees. If we are to follow Jesus as family, then our family tables must also be places of communion with God and one another.

The practice of family table in our homes creates a great environment for connecting at a heart level with one another utilizing the SASHET tool. As we share a meal together, we also share our hearts. Sometimes this a quick meal with only brief opportunity to check in with one another. Other times, we linger over a meal sharing extended time together. This often leads to prayer for one another.

> A few months ago, my middle school age daughter had a particularly difficult day and was sharing her sadness with us. After listening to her and expressing our concern, we took the time to listen to God so that we could share with her what He was saying. God put the words of Psalm 139 on my heart and I prayed them over my daughter. This was a beautiful moment of God communicating His love

and truth to one of His daughters through one of His sons that never would have happened had we not had the practice of family table creating the time and space for real connection. —*Sam*

Family table is not only to be practiced with the household family but also the larger church family. Consider the role that table fellowship played in the account of the early church found in Acts 2. They met daily not just in the Temple courts but also in homes to fellowship over a meal. Table fellowship was so important to the life of the early church that hospitality was a requirement for church leadership. Spiritual leaders in the early church didn't sit around a board room making decisions about programs or teach Biblical lessons in a church building. They invited others to their tables to experience a taste of God's Kingdom. As they broke bread and drank wine, they spoke of King Jesus whose body was broken and whose blood was shed so that we could enter God's Kingdom and sit at His table as His children. What a powerful and beautiful way to experience and teach the Gospel!

We also can make the family table a core environment for spiritual life in our churches. Spiritual leaders can view their tables as places of ministry at which other families and those who don't live in a family can experience the family for which they were created. Small groups can make the family table a core aspect of their group life, meeting not only to study the principles of the Bible, but to live those principles as they share a meal together. Single followers of Jesus can live in spiritual family relationships as they gather around a family table with spiritual brothers, sisters, moms and dads.

If our churches are to function as spiritual families, then the family table must once again become a frequent gathering place for the church. After all, families develop relational patterns based on the environments they live in. If a family only met once a week in a classroom or at a concert, there is no way they could have the depth of relationship that is the result of regular, intimate conversation with God and one another around a family table. Through the practice of family table, an environment can be created that is conducive to healthy family relationships that demonstrate the Kingdom of God.

Reflection

Family as Church

> *"Every Christian family ought to be as it were a little church…"* Jonathan Edwards

How does your family worship together in the home?

How are you involved the spiritual development of your children?

Describe how your family partners together in ministry.

Church as Family

How often do you communicate or spend time with a friend other than your spouse?

Describe your relationships with other followers of Jesus. Who is a spiritual father or mother to you? Who is a spiritual brother or sister? Who is a spiritual son or daughter? Describe how you worship, fellowship, and live on mission with these people.

Chapter 5

STONE FIVE

Centered & Sent

Where Are We to Follow Jesus?

"As you sent me into the world, so I have sent them into the world." John 17:18

"Where are we going" is a critically important question to answer when heading out on a hike, not only in terms of the ultimate destination, but also in selecting the trails that will be traveled en route. When it comes to following Jesus, many people reflect primarily on the heavenly destination of their journey. Many well intentioned, Jesus loving people possess minimal knowledge about the paths that Jesus is leading His followers along en route to the mountaintop of God's Kingdom come in full. If we are to live as Christ's faithful followers, then we need clarity about where Jesus is leading us this side of His return.

Thankfully, Jesus gave us clarity about where the Christian life is to be lived in His high priestly prayer found in John 17:13-18:

> *"But now I am coming to you, and these things I speak in the world, that they may have my joy fulfilled in themselves. I have given them your word, and the world has hated them because they are not of the world, just as I am not of the world. I do not ask that you take them out of the world, but that you keep them from the evil one. They are not of the world, just as I am not of the world. Sanctify them in the truth; your word is truth. As you sent me into the world, so I have sent them into the world."*

Jesus is leading His follower **into the world**. In this passage the "world" is reference to the people and systems that are at odds with the values of God's eternal Kingdom. Let that sink in for a moment.

Jesus is not leading His followers out of the world so that they can be holy. Instead, He has made His followers holy and is leading them into the world. The Christian life is not about getting worldly people to go to sacred spaces so that they can there encounter Jesus. Instead it is about sacred people who have been sent by Jesus going to worldly spaces so that others can encounter Jesus in His people as they go about their regular lives. We refer to this principle of being sent by Jesus into the world as "sentness."

Jesus clearly grounds our "sentness" in His "sentness"— *"As you sent me into the world, so I have sent them into the world."* So to understand how we are to live sent, we must first understand how Jesus was sent.

Incarnation

When speaking of Jesus being sent to the world, Christians use the word "incarnation" which means "taking on flesh." Jesus is fully God, yet He took on flesh and was born as a baby.

> *The Word became flesh and blood, and moved into the neighborhood. We saw the glory with our own eyes, the one-of-a-kind glory, like Father, like Son, Generous inside and out, true from start to finish.* John 1:14 *The Message*

Incarnation is God's means to accomplish His redemptive purpose for humanity. God's plan was that in the flesh of Jesus, His Kingdom would come to earth. In relating to Him, others experience and enter the Kingdom of the Heavens. Though the Incarnation refers primarily to the major event of God becoming human in Jesus' birth, it is also true that the Incarnation did not end at the manger. The Incarnation continued throughout Jesus' earthly life. Jesus' ministry is meant to be understood as an incarnational ministry. He didn't only teach about a way to the Father; He was the Way in flesh. He didn't only teach the truth about God's Kingdom; He embodied the Truth. He didn't only teach about the kind of life we are to live; He was the Life of God in a human being. The way, the truth, the life is a Person! The Incarnation is God's message, sent to humanity in the flesh of Jesus. This makes Jesus the ultimate ambassador, sent from the Kingdom of Heaven to dwell in the kingdom of the world.

Jesus is sending His followers into the world as He was sent— incarnationally. Through the indwelling of the Holy

Spirit, we also have the life of God living within our flesh. We also are ambassadors of God's Kingdom. *"Therefore we are **ambassadors** for Christ, God making his appeal through us. We implore you on behalf of Christ, be reconciled to God."* (2 Corinthians 5:20) An ambassador is a representative from one kingdom who is sent to live in a different kingdom. Followers of Jesus are sent to the world, like Jesus, to declare and demonstrate the Good News of God's Kingdom.

Answering the "where" question of following Jesus as a call into the world rather than a call away from it will have profound implications for what it means to follow Jesus. It certainly has for us.

> One of my good friends in college, John, became a follower of Jesus in high school through the ministry of Young Life. Over spring break, I went home with John and visited his Young Life club. I knew nothing about Young Life. I thought it was some kind of youth group similar to my youth group experience in church. Boy, was I wrong. When we showed up at the home the group was meeting at, I saw a crowd of kids who didn't look like "church kids." Some of them were smoking; their language was rough; and they certainly weren't wearing "church clothes." I immediately thought, "What kind of youth group is this; and where is the leader?" In answer to the thoughts swirling in my head, John brought me over to his leader who was hanging with one of the groups of kids. Right after I met him, someone yelled that club was starting, and this crowd of kids piled into the basement of

the house. It didn't surprise me that everyone was really into the games, skits, and singing; but when the leader got up to speak, I immediately thought "No way! There's no way this group of kids is going to listen to anything he has to say about God." But as that guy explained to the crowd of kids what sin was and our need for a solution to this problem, you could have heard a pin drop. These kids were drinking in his words. After the meeting, I was in a daze. I was both humbled and intrigued. It humbled me that I had judged these teens as being resistant to the Gospel merely based on appearance and behavior. It intrigued me to find out more because what I tasted in the group was what I read about Jesus in the Gospels. I had always been amazed that the "worldly" crowd of Jesus' day— the tax collectors, prostitutes, and other notorious sinners wanted to be around Jesus. Why was that; and why didn't the "worldly crowd" want to hang around with Jesus' church today?

These questions so intrigued me, that I went to work for Young Life after college. I found out that what attracted that "worldly" crowd of high school kids to that basement was the same thing that attracted the "worldly" crowd to Jesus. Someone had lived "sent." Jesus lived sent— intentionally going to people far from God so that He could communicate grace and truth. In the same manner, that Young Life leader who was a follower of Jesus lived sent. He intentionally had gone to a high school to build relationships with teens who were far from

Christ. Apart from someone living sent as Jesus was sent, those teens would never have been in that basement. —*Sam*

WHO IS SENT?

In hearing that story from Sam's formative years, you may think "Great! I'm glad that God is sending His followers into the world to draw people to Himself." If so, that's a great place to start. If you have been part of a church, you probably think of these "sent" people as missionaries – those who are sent to evangelize other people in other parts of world. But Jesus is not ONLY sending professional missionaries into the world. Listen to His words in John 17:20 that identify who is He is sending: *"I am praying not only for these disciples but also for all who will ever believe in me through their message."*(NLT)

ALL who believe in Jesus are being sent into the world. "Sentness" is an essential component of what it means to follow Jesus. If we lack sentness, we miss out on where Jesus is leading His followers today. Jesus gave us His Spirit so that we would "live sent" in the world as witness to the life of Jesus that resides within every disciple (Acts 1:8).

Now, a necessary corrective is needed here. Our western ears almost always hear this call to live sent as an individual call. While sentness does involve individual responsibility, it is primarily to be understood as a community undertaking. Look at John 17:21 *"that they may all be one, just as you, Father, are in me, and I in you, that they also may be in us, so that the world may believe that you have sent* me." Followers of Jesus are to live sent *together,* so that the world sees not only individual Christians but the community of Christ. As followers of Jesus live sent together, there is power that results from the diversity of gifting and unity of the Spirit found in their midst. Our greatest apologetic is the life of God in His people producing unity that is not of this world. The only way the world is going to see this reality is if the community of Jesus lives sent together.

Have you ever thought of yourself as a missionary or thought of your church as a missional community? According to Jesus, God is sending His church into the world, therefore we are all missionaries. He is sending His people together into the world so that His Kingdom might come and His will be done on earth as it is in Heaven. Together, we are sent to bless the world, to demonstrate the values of His Kingdom, and invite others to receive citizenship within the gracious Kingdom of our Lord Jesus.

The Heart of Sentness

Jesus' followers are sent as Jesus was sent. The same motivation that compelled the Father to send the Son compels Jesus to send His followers. John 3:16-17 speaks of this motivation:

> *For God so loved the world, that he gave his only Son, that whoever believes in him should not perish but have eternal life. For God did not send his Son into the world to condemn the world, but in order that the world might be saved through him.*

It does no good to live sent, if we do not have God's heart. If we are motivated by desires to prove ourselves or to impress others, we will likely do more harm than good. We must be reminded again and again that what sent Jesus to earth was God's great love for humanity. God loved the world that hated Him. God loved the world that rejected Him. God loved the world that crucified His Son. God loved the world then; God loves the world now. God loved so expansively, so completely that Jesus was willing to die.

As Christians, we are quite familiar with the idea that Jesus loved sinful people enough to die for them, but we often forget that He loved sinful people enough to befriend them. In Luke 15, we find a typical encounter between Jesus and the religious leaders who didn't understand God's heart for those who live far from Him.

> *Tax collectors and other notorious sinners often came to listen to Jesus teach. This made the Pharisees and teachers of religious law complain that he was associating with such sinful people— even eating with them!* Luke 15:1-2 NLT

To eat with someone in the culture of Jesus' day was to accept them, to befriend them, to declare them valuable. It was understandable that Jesus might want to preach to sinful people. Who knows, maybe they'll repent? But to accept them and befriend them while they were still sinners was too much for these proud, self-righteous people to bear. Jesus' friendship with "sinners" caused the religious leaders to characterize Him as a glutton, drunkard, and an unapologetic friend of sinners. This reputation didn't seem to bother Jesus in the least. Our Savior wasn't motivated by a desire to prove himself or impress others. He was motivated by the heart of God that loves the world. He described this motivation in responding to the religious leader's objection as to His relationships. Jesus told three stories about three things that were of great value, were lost, and then found.

The first story involved a solitary sheep who strayed from the rest of the herd. The shepherd left the ninety-nine other sheep and searched for the one lost lamb until it was found. Then He carried it home and threw a party to celebrate the sheep's safe return. The second story involved a lost coin that a woman searched diligently for until it was found. Then, she also threw a party to celebrate her precious coin being found. The last story involved a lost son who returned home and who also was greeted with a festive celebration. In these stories, Jesus is describing God's heart and explaining His own ministry. God's heart is filled with deep love for the "notorious sinners" that the religious leaders arrogantly sought to avoid. Because of God's love, Jesus sought out these people and ate with them. Through table fellowship, He was extending the grace of God. These meals with notorious sinners weren't just an evangelism strategy that He grudgingly endured. His friendships with broken people brought genuine joy to Jesus' heart. He delighted in the festive celebrations they shared together.

If we are to live sent into the world as Jesus was sent, we also must be motivated by the deep love of God that sent Jesus into the world that God loves. Living sent will mean not just telling people the message of Jesus, but befriending them. Through developing friendships, the love of God takes on real flesh and moves into our actual neighborhood.

The Methods of Sentness

Now, some Christians really do have God's heart for the world, yet lack winsomeness in living sent. These followers of Jesus desire that other people come to experience the kingdom of Jesus, but are often abrasive in how they go about living sentness. Especially when it comes to sentness, it isn't enough to be sincere if we are to effectively live on mission with Jesus among those whom aren't yet aware that our Father is drawing them to Himself. Let's examine Paul's instructions to the Jesus followers in ancient Colossae:

> Walk in wisdom toward outsiders, making the best use of the time. Let your speech always be gracious, seasoned with salt, so that you may know how you ought to answer each person.
> Colossians 4:5-6

Wisdom and winsomeness are the result of living sent as Jesus was sent. The same manner of ministry that Jesus employed is to be ours as well. Let us explore some of the characteristics of Jesus' way of living sent.

Life on Life Relationship

Jesus genuinely cared for people and therefore invested himself relationally in those to whom He was sent. Consider the story of Zacchaeus the tax collector found in Luke 19:1-10.

> He entered Jericho and was passing through. And behold, there was a man named Zacchaeus. He was a chief tax collector and was rich. And he was seeking to see who Jesus was, but on account of the crowd he could not, because he was small in stature. So he ran on ahead and climbed up into a sycamore tree to see him, for he was about to pass that way. And when Jesus came to the place, he looked up and said to him, "Zacchaeus, hurry and come down, for I must stay at your house today." So he hurried and came down and received him joyfully. And when they saw it, they all grumbled, "He has gone in to be the guest of a man who is a sinner." And Zacchaeus stood and said to the Lord, "Behold, Lord, the half of my goods I give to the poor. And if I have defrauded anyone of anything, I restore it fourfold." And Jesus said to him, "Today salvation has come to this house, since he also is a son of Abraham. For the Son of Man came to seek and to save the lost."

In this account we see Jesus' relational pattern of ministry clearly demonstrated. Notice first that a large crowd had gathered together to see what the famous rabbi from Nazareth would do. Even though Jesus loved the crowds and often taught them, Jesus did not feel the need to give this particular crowd His time or attention. He chose instead to invest hours over a dinner with a man that the crowd despised. Over the din of the crowd, Jesus called to Zacchaeus by name. In that moment, Zaccheus realized that he was known by the Savior. How both wonderful and terrifying it must have been for Zacchaeus to realize that he was known by the sage of Galilee!

Notice next that Jesus didn't give Zaccheus either a sermon or a scolding, instead He invited Himself over to Zach's for dinner! This may sound rude to us today, but it was considered the highest of honors that could be shown to Zacchaeus. Jesus was publicly announcing his acceptance of and friendship with the reviled tax collector. In that instant, the thieving runt of the litter was no longer the object of the community's scorn but the focus of its combined envy. Jesus' relational investment in Zacchaeus was an act of sheer grace. Even though Zacchaeus did not deserve this attention and affirmation, Jesus decided to extend it to him anyway. Zacchaeus life was radically transformed by the grace of Jesus expressed to him through relationship.

We are called to live our sentness with the same kind of relational priority. We also need to invest ourselves in developing life-on-life relationships. People need to feel the grace of Jesus through our acceptance and friendship. If we view people as speed bumps or pit stops that slow us down from the real work of ministry that needs to be done, then we miss the entire point of Jesus' command to live sent. People are the objects of God's grace and mercy and if we are to follow Jesus into the world, then we must thoroughly immerse ourselves in actual life-on-life relationships with real, hurting, and broken people.

Tangible Blessing

When we read about the life of Jesus in the Gospel accounts, we see that he not only cared for people's souls, but their bodies as well. He healed, fed, and cared for people's bodies because He genuinely cares about the real, everyday needs that real, everyday people face. His Kingdom is not only a "spiritual kingdom" that consists of religious ideas while ignoring all other areas of life; His Kingdom reigns over every aspect of life!

When He sent out His disciples on their first missionary journey, He gave them these instructions: *"Heal the sick, and say to them, 'The Kingdom of God has come near to you.'"* (Luke 10:9) The rule of Jesus became apparent as tangible needs were met in Christ's power. After all, the future fulfillment of Jesus' Kingdom is the tangible healing of all things. Our bodies will be made new (1 Corinthians 15) and our world will be made new (Revelation 21). When we meet tangible needs in the name of Jesus, we are helping others to experience the Kingdom of God that will one day remake everything to be somehow even better than the original perfect creation of our God.

History records that followers of Jesus took this aspect of "tangible blessing" very seriously. The followers of Jesus who lived in Rome during the great plague of 260AD, stayed in the city caring for the sick and dying while the rest of the great city's residents fled in terror to save their own lives. This kind of "tangible blessing" was so characteristic of the first Christians that the emperor Julian complained to the pagan high priest of Galatia in a letter written in 362 that *"The impious Galileans support not only their poor, but ours as well, everyone can see that our people lack aid from us.*"[22] It's no wonder that the Gospel of Jesus so radically swept through the ancient world. The blessings of this Gospel were so often conveyed in tangible ways that it caused that the good news to permeate nearly every social strata of the Roman Empire.

We are to follow Jesus and the Christians who have gone before us in bringing tangible blessing to people. This will take the form of working for justice in our world in ways such as providing for the poor, caring for orphans, and ministering to the sick. It will also take the form of creating beautiful glimpses into God's Kingdom through art, music, and film. By addressing in tangible ways what is wrong in this world and creating beautiful glimpses of God's Kingdom, we are joining Jesus in His mission of reconciliation and renewal that He will complete when He returns and fully establishes His Kingdom.

Gracious Truth

Investing in people relationally and meeting tangible needs is crucial to living sent, but it isn't everything. The Gospel must be demonstrated by action AND proclaimed with words. Paul wrote in Romans 10:14, "*But how can they call on him to save them unless they believe in him? And how can they believe in him if they have never heard about him? And how can they hear about him unless someone tells them?*" (NLT) People enter God's Kingdom, not by enjoying the blessings of the Kingdom, but by entering relationship with the King. For that to happen, a verbal introduction is required.

In His ministry, Jesus not only befriended people and cared for tangible needs, He also *"went on through cities and villages, proclaiming and bringing the good news of the Kingdom of God"* (Luke 8:1). Jesus demonstrated God's Kingdom through tangible means. He also proclaimed that He was the King and that people could enter His Kingdom by believing in Him and becoming His follower. This method of "demonstration" and "proclamation" can be seen in Jesus' encounter with the Samaritan woman found in John 4. Jesus met this woman at her town well during the middle of day. Jesus crossed the cultural barriers of gender and ethnicity and struck up conversation with her. This demonstrated the love of God's Kingdom.

As He talked with this woman, He revealed that though He had never met her before, He knew she had been married five times and was currently living with a man to whom she wasn't married. The woman rightly recognized that Jesus was "a prophet." Jesus' insight into her life had been a revelation from God demonstrating the "nearness of God's Kingdom." Interestingly, the conversation then became about mountains— whether to worship God on the Samaritan mountain of Gerizim or the Temple Mount in Jerusalem. Jesus pointed her to the ultimate Kingdom hope, that one day worship would not be confined to the mountain in Samaria or Jerusalem. The woman knew what Jesus talking about because she responded that when the Messiah came He would tell us "all things." Jesus then introduced her to the Messianic King who will rule from mountain of the Lord, "I who speak to you am He."

In this interaction, notice how necessary it was that Jesus was both gracious in his actions and truthful with his words. Unfortunately, many people pit gracious actions and truthful words against one another. Even within the Christian church there is often division between those demonstrating God's Kingdom through deeds of grace and those declaring God's Kingdom through words of truth. Leslie Newbigin summed this silly bifurcation up well when he said:

> So, for God's sake, let us not fall into this game of setting words and deeds against each other, preaching against action for justice and action for justice against preaching. Do not let us set "kingdom" against "church" and "church" against "kingdom." The church is not an end in itself. "Church growth" is not an end in itself. The church is only true to its calling when it is a sign, an instrument and a foretaste of the kingdom. But, on the other hand, talk about the kingdom is mere ideology if it is not tied to the name of Jesus in whom the kingdom is present and if it does not invite men and women to recognize that presence, to do the U-turn, to become part of that company that (sinful as it has always been) acknowledges Jesus as the one in whom God's kingdom is present and so seeks to honor him, to serve him, to follow him.[23]

Sadly, we find it difficult to be both truthful and gracious. Some find it easier to speak truth than show grace. They have an attitude that says "I'm right, you're wrong, and I would love to tell you about it." Truth without grace comes off as harsh arrogance and often turns people away. Others find it easier to show grace than speak truth. People love to be around them because they are friendly and very rarely cause offense. However, their graciousness rarely leads to other's transformation for it lacks the clear truth that is needed. Jesus was *"full of grace and truth"* (John 1:14). Connected to Him, we have access to both the grace and truth that we need to live sent.

Humble Sacrifice

Living sent like Jesus requires us to invest in life-on-life relationships, demonstrate tangible blessing, and speak gracious truth, but those aspects of sentness will be empty and powerless if not characterized by humble sacrifice like Jesus. We would go so far as to say it is impossible to be sent as Jesus was sent if we do not humbly sacrifice as He humbly sacrificed. Philippians 2:6-8 describes how Jesus was sent, *"though he was in the form of God, did not count equality with God a thing to be grasped, but emptied himself, by taking the form of a servant, being born in the likeness of men. And being found in human form, he humbled himself by becoming obedient to the point of death, even death on a cross."* Jesus did not cling to His status or comfort when He was sent. His ministry was not marked by riches, fame, or success. Instead, He humbly endured poverty, suffering, and death. We cannot understand Jesus' sentness apart from the cross, and we cannot follow Him without taking up our own. Jesus said as much: *"If anyone would come after me, let him deny himself and take up his cross daily and follow me."* Leslie

Newbigin highlights the catalytic role of humble sacrifice in Christian mission:

> *Let us never forget that in its first and mightiest conflict against the powers of this world, represented in the imperial might of Rome, the victory of the gospel was won not by the cleverness of its preachers and theologians, and certainly not by its programs for social justice, but by the blood of the martyrs. And let us not forget that the most notable examples of vital Christian mission today are to be found in places where success in worldly terms has been denied.*[24]

Sentness in the way of Jesus is the way of the cross. Yes this will require "big" sacrifices at times. Being sent like Jesus may mean sacrificing a career, financial security, approval of family, or even life itself. But when Jesus invited His disciples to "take up their crosses" he invited them (and us) to do so *DAILY*. Many of us wonder how we could ever be able to make a "big sacrifice" to follow Jesus as so many of the "heroes" of the faith have done. We may read through examples in the Bible or hear missionary stories and think that those were special people unlike us. But that is not the case. They were ordinary men and women who had daily taken up their crosses in the everyday places of life and made humble sacrifice their lifestyle. Daily, they set aside their wills in favor of God's will. In their homes, neighborhoods, and places of work they consistently set aside their natural inclination to live for their own comfort, pleasure, and glory in favor of God's kingdom, righteous, and glory. They were able to live sent at all costs because they learned to take up their cross daily in the everyday places of life.

The result of humble sacrifice is the multiplication of new life. Jesus said about His own sacrifice that *"unless a grain of wheat falls into the earth and dies, it remains alone; but if it dies, it bears much fruit."* (John 12:24) God has written the catalytic power of sacrifice into the fabric of this earth. Every fall, as the cold of the coming winter begins to overtake the trees of New England, their leaves become glorious in death. As these trees drop their dying leaves, they also drop thousands of seeds that sink into the ground. With the coming of spring, these fertile seeds burst forth from the earth as the tender shoots of new trees.

Harriet Beecher Stowe created a moving picture of the power of sacrifice in her classic Uncle Tom's Cabin. The main character, Tom, humbly lived out the teachings of Jesus. He served his enemies and refused to return evil for evil and was murdered as a result. Yet, his sacrifice became the catalyst for others salvation and freedom. Listen to Stowe's beautiful words about people like Tom: *"There are in this world blessed souls, whose sorrows all spring up into joys for others; whose earthly hopes, laid in the grave with many tears, are the seed from which spring healing flowers and balm for the desolate and the distressed."*

Make no mistake dear friend, sentness in the way of Jesus always requires humble sacrifice. It is not possible to be sent like Jesus without taking up our cross. Yes, living sent will hurt, but living sent is worth the cost incurred. Jesus' grievous death resulted in His glorious resurrection which has in turn offered the opportunity to experience new life to untold millions. As His followers take up their crosses, Jesus promises that we too will experience His resurrection life and be part of multiplying it to countless others.

Centeredness Results in Sentness

The outcome of sentness is Kingdom expansion. As followers of Jesus live sent, more people enter the reign of Jesus and come to live under His gracious rule. This was the vision that first captivated the Missional Architect group that developed the Five Stones. We desperately wanted to see followers of Jesus living sent lives that by God's grace would result in the spontaneous expansion of the church.

Yet, along the way, we sensed that something was missing if this vision was to be realized. The call to live sent is hollow all by itself. Many disciples desire to "live sent" but feel inadequate and guilty. Simply trying harder to do more for Jesus and say more about Jesus rarely leads to fruitful ministry. That is because sentness is a **fruit**. You can't willpower fruit into growing. It grows simply because it is connected to the vine. Jesus told His followers *"I am the vine; you are the branches. Whoever abides in me and I in him, he it is that bears much fruit, for apart from me you can do nothing."* (John 15:5) How wonderful to realize that Jesus didn't call His followers to bear fruit by their own power. He intends to fill them with His life and energy that results in fruitful ministry.

Yet, we are not to be passive in this process. Jesus told us to "abide" in Him in order that we might bear much fruit. This "abiding" is about having our lives "centered" in Jesus. He is to be central to all that we do. When we are centered in Jesus, sentness is the result. Centered in Jesus, our work naturally becomes an avenue of sentness. Centered in Jesus, our families naturally becomes communities of sentness. Centered in Jesus, our hobbies naturally become environments of sentness.

So, how do we live centered? We've already described the pathway. The principles and practices of Stone One through Stone Four describe a life centered in Jesus.

Stone One: What are we to do as we follow Jesus?

Principle: Love God, Love Others,
and Make Disciples

Vertical Practice: Connect at a heart level with the
Lord through the Scriptures

Horizontal Practice: Connect at a heart level with
one another through SASHET

Stone Two: How are we to follow Jesus?

Principle: The Leadership of the Holy Spirit

Vertical Practice: Listening Prayer

Horizontal Practice: Speaking God's words
to others

Stone Three: When are we to follow Jesus?

Principle: Daily Rhythms

Vertical Practice: Morning prayer of Dedication

Horizontal Practice: Rhythms of rest— worship,
generosity, and celebration

Stone Four: With Whom are we to follow Jesus?

Principle: Family is church, Church is family

Vertical Practice: Family Worship

Horizontal Practice: Family Table

Trying to live sent without being centered in Jesus is like salt that has lost its taste. It is useless, good for nothing except to be thrown out and trampled (Matthew 5:13). Therefore, if we want to live sent by Jesus, we must give ourselves to living centered in Jesus. The principles and practices described in the first four stones must become our authentic way of life. This way of life in Christ naturally leads to sentness for He produces in us the power to live sent. Jesus also produces for us the unique situations into which we are sent. The progression of grace looks like this; We abide in Him, He bears fruit in us. We center our lives in Him, He sends us out on His mission.

When sentness flows from centeredness in Jesus our activity will flow from God's heart not our own agendas for success or self-glory. Once again, Newbigin speaks to the very heart of this issue when he says:

> *Success in the sense of growth in the number of committed Christians is not in our hands. It is the work of God the Holy Spirit to call men and women to faith in Jesus, and the Spirit does so in ways that are often mysterious and beyond any possibility of manipulation or even of comprehension by us. What is required of us is faithfulness in word and deed, at whatever cost; faithfulness in action for truth, for justice, for mercy, for compassion; faithfulness*

in speaking the name of Jesus when the time is right, bearing witness, by explicit word as occasion arises, to God whose we are and whom we serve. There are situations where the word is easy and the deed is costly; there are situations where the deed is easy and the word is costly. Whether in word or in deed, what is required in every situation is that we be faithful to him who said to his disciples: "As the Father sent me, so I send you," and showed them his hands and his side.[25]

Sentness that flows from centeredness makes us able to persevere through seasons of discouragement and difficulty. It also makes us humble and gracious during seasons of "success." When we are centered in Jesus— He is our goal. Whether we are comfortable or suffering; successful or discouraged; happy or sad; rich or poor— like Paul we say *"I want to know Christ and experience the mighty power that raised him from the dead. I want to suffer with him, sharing in his death, so that one way or another I will experience the resurrection from the dead!"* (Philippians 3:10-11 NLT)

While we believe that sentness is a fruit of centeredness, we also believe that sentness must be cultivated. We need not only a heart centered in Jesus, but the ability to see what God is doing around us and the skill set necessary to join Him in His work. Therefore, we need practices that will help us live sent.

VERTICAL PRACTICE:
Missional Prayer

When Jesus sent His disciples on mission, He instructed them to "pray to the Lord of the harvest." Prayer is essential because Jesus' disciples do not labor *for* Jesus, but *with* Him. In prayer, the heart of the one being sent is cultivated to be sensitive to where Jesus is already at work. And in prayer, we are asking Jesus to prepare the hearts of those to whom He is sending us.

> I've experienced how central prayer is to sentness. This past year, a good friend of mine who isn't a Christian lost one of his dogs. This dog is incredibly special to him and his family. He invested himself completely in the search for his much loved dog. One day as I was driving, I was praying for my friend. As I prayed, God powerfully impressed on me how my friend's search for his dog represented God's search for us. I immediately thought of Luke 15 and the story of the Shepherd who lost a sheep, the woman who lost a coin, and the Father who lost a son. This realization of God's heart touched me deeply, but I immediately sensed God was impressing this on me so that I could share it with my friend. I fought this. It seemed weird and I wasn't sure how my friend would react. But after a week of hesitation, I sent him an e-mail expressing my concern for his family and what God had put on my heart to share with him. Far from being offended, he also sensed that something significant was happening in his life

during this experience of searching for his lost dog. This led to an evening at a local pub talking about his story and the larger story of God. —*Sam*

Prayer was the catalyst for that conversation to even happen. In prayer, God showed me what He was doing in my friend's life. In prayer my heart was enlarged to care about what God cares about. Through prayer, God sent me to be an encouragement and a witness to my friend. Mission flows from prayer.

A good way to practice missional prayer is to regularly ask God two questions:

1. *God, where are you at work in this place/with these people?*
2. *God, how can I join You in what You are doing?*

These two questions come from Henry Blackaby's book *Experiencing God* which highlight two extremely helpful truths. First, God is always at work around us. Secondly, God invites us to become personally involved with Him in His work. Therefore, it is a helpful practice to pray these two prayers as we go to work, school, or community activities.

HORIZONTAL PRACTICE:
Residential Living and Hospitality

The story of St Patrick is a striking example of this practice. St Patrick was born in Britain into a fairly wealthy family around the year 387 AD. At the age of 16 he was kidnapped from Britain by Irish raiders and taken as a slave back to Ireland, which at that time was a land ruled by a cruel and barbaric tribal system.

Patrick was held captive in Ireland as a slave for six years before he escaped. But during those six years, God became real to Him and began to change his heart. So much so, that after he escaped and fled back to Britain, he couldn't stop thinking about the Irish people who had enslaved him. Instead of anger and bitterness, he felt compassion toward them and sensed God leading him to return to Ireland to serve these pagan people and help them come to encounter the very same Jesus who had so changed his heart and life.

Patrick returned to Ireland with a community of friends. This community would live in close enough proximity to an Irish village that their Christian way of life was seen. They blessed the Irish people in tangible ways and invited them to experience their way of life in Christ. Through this ministry, thousands of Irish people came to experience the love and grace of Jesus. Patrick and his team of Jesus followers changed the whole future course of Irish history and culture as they lived joyfully submitted to King Jesus.

Residential Living

Sentness requires that we "reside" among those to whom God is sending us in a similar way to how Patrick resided among the Irish. We are sent as residential missionaries to our neighborhoods, community sports, schools, and workplaces so that Christ can be seen and experienced through our lives. Both of us have experienced God's call to live as a residential missionary over the past few years.

One of the most intimate encounters I have ever had with God occurred at the one stoplight in our town. While waiting in my Subaru wagon I heard the Holy Spirit speak the following words into my soul; "You don't have any real friends who aren't already following me." It was a devastating moment as I vainly flipped through my internal mental catalog that contained the friends that I have accumulated across the country. The truth was shocking. My own spirit affirmed the truthfulness of the revelation I had just received from the Spirit of God. Amidst my tears, I realized that I wasn't living in any kind of real relationship with anyone who existed outside the body of Christ. In that moment of both epiphany and shame, I committed myself to find substantial ways to share my life with the pre-Christian people that lived in my town and region. This resolve sent me on a journey that saw me join a veterans group, our village's planning committee and my local volunteer fire department. All of this was new and initially uncomfortable territory for me.

I requested to be interviewed for membership at the Voorheesville Volunteer Fire Dept. The night of the meeting I was asked why exactly I wanted to join their ranks. Did I know that they already had a chaplain to fill any spiritual needs that emerged? I told my interviewers that I wanted to ride the truck and serve the community alongside them, not to be a another chaplain. Looks of disbelief and then smiles of affirmation broke out. The membership of the fire department agreed to allow me entrance and I preceded "to do life" with them. It has been incredibly life-giving to hone my newly acquired firefighting skills, respond to fires, floods and accidents with them. I have enjoyed hanging out with a number of them socially and in pursuit of fraternal service to our community outside of responding to "the tones." Although a number of them have shared that while they aren't looking to be converted, they do appreciate my friendship and service to our community. Quite a few of them have attended a number of special services our church has held to honor emergency service volunteers in our community. One of the men who isn't a religious person told me after one of these services that though he didn't like churches "I like this church." My friend went on to say that the reason he wasn't real fond of christian people was because of some of the caustic attempts to convert him that he had experienced in his past. I am praying that this friend of mine and his wife will join us regularly at some point in the near future.

My willingness to share my life and family with the men I purposely live amongst has given me many many opportunities to meet, listen to and serve people that would never come to my church otherwise. In a strange but beautiful twist of God's providence, I find that these men and women who have yet to trust Christ with their lives often become the unknowing conduits through which the Spirit of Jesus ministers to me. Its all about proximity and a willingness to love without expectation of return. —*Foye*

Hospitality

Sentness also requires hospitality. Just as Patrick invited the Irish into his community before they became Christians, we must extend rich hospitality to those to whom we are sent as well. When you read through the New Testament Scripture, notice how often hospitality is mentioned as being an outflow of the Gospel (and a requirement for church leadership). Hospitality is a tangible expression of the Gospel.

My family has practiced hospitality by throwing a St Patrick's Day party on a couple of occasions. We invite a number of friends over, some of whom are followers of Jesus, some who are not. As we enjoy some corn beef and Guinness, I hand out a number of Irish jokes and blessings that are read. After that, I tell the story of St. Patrick and how it reveals the story of Jesus. I always love those parties. I love enjoying the gift of food and fellowship among people who are at very different places in their faith journey. I love seeing people connect with one another and unexpectedly encounter the message and life of Jesus. Usually at some point in the evening, I find myself looking around the room and thinking "such is the Kingdom." Jesus is advancing

His Kingdom in this world now through seemingly insignificant acts of hospitality, compassion, and witness. In those moments I pray that those sitting at my table will also be sitting with me at God's table in the future Kingdom. —Sam

One day when Christ returns, we will feast at the King's table. We will dwell upon the mountain top and enjoy God's Kingdom, newly arrived in all its glorious fullness. This world will be filled with the knowledge of God and His glory. Until that day, Jesus is leading His followers into the world to live centered and sent. Yes, this involves discomfort and difficulty. So we must remind ourselves of what is true. Jesus is ruling now and will one day return and heaven and earth will be united. The hymn "This Is My Father's World beautifully capture this reality:

> *This is my Father's world.*
> *O let me ne'er forget*
>
> *That though the wrong seems oft so strong,*
> *God is the ruler yet.*
>
> *This is my Father's world:*
> *the battle is not done:*
>
> *Jesus Who died shall be satisfied,*
> *And earth and Heaven be one.*

Until that day, Jesus is sending us into His world as "co-laborers" with Him in the advance of His Kingdom in this age. So as we follow Jesus we pray, "Your Kingdom come, Your will be done on earth as it is in heaven."

Reflection

You are the salt of the earth, but if salt has lost its taste, how shall its saltiness be restored? It is no longer good for anything except to be thrown out and trampled under people's feet.You are the light of the world. A city set on a hill cannot be hidden. Nor do people light a lamp and put it under a basket, but on a stand, and it gives light to all in the house. In the same way, let your light shine before others, so that they may see your good works and give glory to your Father who is in heaven.
Matthew 5:13-16

"Salt" has to do with good deeds that are the "flavor" of Jesus' Kingdom in your life. Lives that are "salty" are a result of living centered in Jesus. "Light" has to do with the visibility of the good deeds that demonstrate Jesus' Kingdom. Lives that are "light" are a result of living sent by Jesus. In light of this, consider the following questions:

To where and to whom is God sending you as an ambassador of His Kingdom? How are you seeking to demonstrate the Kingdom of God in that place/with those people.

What barriers or obstacles keep you from living as "salt and light"? How might God be calling you to address those?

Conclusion

What do I do Next?

Now that you've made it through the book, what next? How can the Five Stones become your way of life in Christ rather being just more Christian information?

Make practice not just information your aim

Most of our education, both inside and outside the church, measures the amount of information gained, but information by itself is useless unless applied to life. Church libraries are full of books that have been read without having much effect in the actual lives of real people. Reading this book and learning information about the Five Stones will be useless unless you rehearse the practices and begin developing a way of life. So, look at the vertical and horizontal practices for each stone. Start by implementing the practices from Stone One into your life. Make a plan for when and how you will do the practices. As you develop consistency in the Stone One practices, add in the practices from Stone Two and so on and so forth.

Experiment and contextualize

We encourage you to experiment with the practices as you implement them into your life. Everyone needs to figure out for themselves how to implement the practices based on their schedule, personality, and family situation. I know of many different ways families live the practices. That's a good thing. Sam's family loves to say the affirmations for Stone One each morning at breakfast. Not every family needs to do that. Foye's family checks in using SASHET every evening. Others check in with extended family over a video chat once a week. Some groups gather together weekly in homes as a larger family. Others gather monthly for the same purpose. Some groups are sent to make disciples of middle school students in their community. Others are sent to Germany to begin new communities. The principles of the Five Stones do not change, but how they are practiced should be adapted to meet the needs of the various cultures to which they are brought. In doing so, this way of life can be lived among all people everywhere.

Practice in community

To learn and live this way of life you must commit yourself to a community. It is impossible to live this way of life by yourself. This may be the most difficult part for many. It may be inconvenient and scary to devote yourself to practicing this way of life in community. Yet, this journey must be walked with other travelers. So identify who it is that Jesus is calling you to journey with and devote yourself to a way of life together.

Teach others

The goal is not only for you to follow Jesus, but for the whole world to be filled with God's Kingdom and His glory. You are part of making that happen as you live this way of life and teach others. Teach your family and friends even as you are learning. Invite others to "tastes" of Jesus in your way of living. As they learn to live the Five Stones, teach them to teach others. It is really that simple.

The Five Stones:
An Everyday Guide to Following Jesus

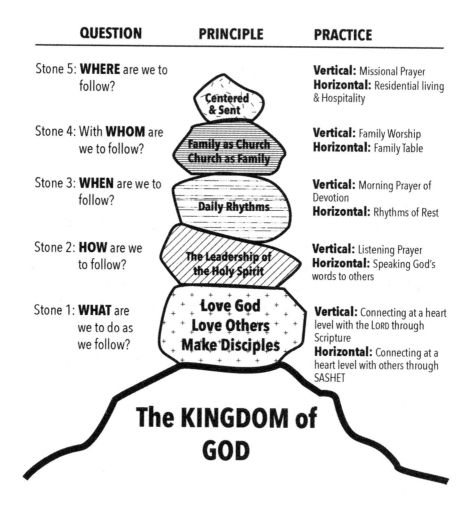

QUESTION	PRINCIPLE	PRACTICE

Stone 5: **WHERE** are we to follow?

Centered & Sent

Vertical: Missional Prayer
Horizontal: Residential living & Hospitality

Stone 4: With **WHOM** are we to follow?

Family as Church Church as Family

Vertical: Family Worship
Horizontal: Family Table

Stone 3: **WHEN** are we to follow?

Daily Rhythms

Vertical: Morning Prayer of Devotion
Horizontal: Rhythms of Rest

Stone 2: **HOW** are we to follow?

The Leadership of the Holy Spirit

Vertical: Listening Prayer
Horizontal: Speaking God's words to others

Stone 1: **WHAT** are we to do as we follow?

Love God Love Others Make Disciples

Vertical: Connecting at a heart level with the LORD through Scripture
Horizontal: Connecting at a heart level with others through SASHET

The KINGDOM of GOD

Epilogue

What is the Vision for the Five Stones?

We believe that Christianity is a way of life based on belief.[26] In the past, the church has done good and important work clarifying the essential beliefs of the Christian faith. In the present, we believe that the church must clarify and emphasize the way of life that Jesus is calling His followers to live. Rick Warren told the Baptist World Alliance in 2005:

> I'm looking for a second reformation. The first reformation of the church 500 years ago was about beliefs. This one is going to be about behavior. The first one was about creeds. This one is going to be about deeds. It is not going to be about what does the church believe, but about what is the church doing.[27]

We agree. We desire a reformation of practice in the way of Jesus. We believe the Five Stones can help clarify the way of life in Christ and equip people to follow Jesus in the everyday places of life.

We desire that the Five Stones would be used to help existing churches of all styles and structures become revitalized as they learn not only a way of belief and religious attendance, but discover a way of life in Christ together.

We also desire that the Five Stones be used to help new disciple-making communities form based on a way of life in Christ. The simplicity of the Five Stones makes it highly adaptable for use in a variety of settings.

Finally, and most importantly, we desire that the Five Stones be used to help families learn to live a way of life in Christ together. If Christianity is to flourish in the West, it will not be through the attractiveness of church structures and programs but through the vibrancy of Christ's life shining through ordinary families in the everyday places of life.

We invite you to join us in living this way of life in Christ.

Endnotes

Prologue

[1] Ladd, George Eldon. *The Gospel Of The Kingdom*. Grand Rapids: Wm. B. Eerdmans Publishing Company, 1990. p. 19.

[2] Johnston, Tom & Perkinson, Mike. *The Organic Reformation*. Manchester Praxis Media, 2009. p. 48.

[3] Bunyan, John. The Pilgrim's Progress. London. 1874-76. p. 55.

[4] Lewis, CS. The Last Battle. New York: Collier Books. 1970. p. 171.

Chapter 1— *Love God, Love Others, Make Disciples*

[5] Johnston, Tom and Perkinson, Mike. *The Organic Reformation*. Manchester, Praxis Media 2009. p.30.

[6] Peterson, Andrew. The Monster In The Hallows. Nashville, TN: Rabbit Room Press 2011.

[7] Hewett, James S. *Illustrations Unlimited*. Wheaton: Tyndale House Publishers, Inc, 1988. p. 178.

[8] Johnston, Tom. *The Way Of The Master*. 2013 p. 24.

[9] Willard, Dallas. *The Great Omission*. Harper Collins 2006.

[10] Lewis, C.S. *Mere Christianity*. New York, Simon & Schuster Touchstone, 1996. p. 171.

Chapter 2— *The Leadership of the Holy Spirit*

[11] Thomas, Ian. *The Indwelling Life of Christ*. Multnomah Books, 2006. p 8.

[12] Grudem, Wayne. *Systematic Theology,* Grand Rapids:. Zondervan, 1994. p. 1050.

[13] Strand, Greg. *Evangelical Convictions*. Minneapolis: Free Church Publications, 2011. p. 151.

[14] David W. Pao http://efcatoday.org/story/god-speaks.

[15] Tozer, AW. *The Pursuit of God*. ReadaClassic.com. 2010. p 7.

Chapter 3— *Daily Rhythms*

[16] Peterson, Eugene. *A Long Obedience In The Same Direction*. Downers Grove, IL: InterVarsity Pres 2000.

[17] Hoag, Gary. *Outcomes Magazine*, Fall 2012, p. 17.

[18] Lewis, C.S. *Mere Christianity*. New York, Simon & Schuster Touchstone, 1996.

Chapter 4— *Family as Church, Church as Family*

19 Keller, Timothy. *The Prodigal God.* New York, Riverhead Books. 2008.

20 Edwards, Johnathan. *Farwell Sermon: The Works of Jonathan Edwards*, Vol. I, p. ccvi.

21 Jones, Sally Lloyd. *The Jesus Storybook Bible.* Zonderkidz. 2007.

Chapter 5— *Centered & Sent*

22 quoted in Johnson 1976:75; Ayerst and Fisher 1971:179-181). [ibid. pp. 83-84, par. 5 & 1 resp.]

23 Newbigin, Leslie. *Mission in Christ's Way.* Geneva: WCC Publications, 1987. p. 12-13.

24 Newbigin, Leslie. *Mission in Christ's Way.* Geneva: WCC Publications, 1987. p. 13-14.

25 Newbigin, Leslie. *Mission in Christ's Way.* Geneva: WCC Publications, 1987. p. 12-13.

Epilogue

26 Johnston, Tom and Perkinson, Mike. *The Organic Reformation.* Manchester, Praxis Media 2009.

27 Warren, Rick 2005 Message at the Baptist World Alliance. *http://www.beliefnet.com/ Faiths/Christianity/2005/10/Rick-Warrens- SecondReformation.aspx#3yZH6HU6KiEc2y58.99*

About the Authors

Foye Belyea is passionate about helping the body of Christ build bridges that bring about Gospel transformation in their communities. He is the pastor of Mountainview Church in Voorheesville, NY. He and his wife Maria have two children and one mini-schnauzer.

Sam Huggard has a deep desire to see ordinary men and women who are far from God made into extraordinary followers of Jesus. He pastors BeFree Community Church- Alton which he planted in 2006. He and his wife Wendy live in Alton, New Hampshire with their three children.

For more information visit:
http://the5stones.org